The Mystery of Christ

The Mystery of Christ

The Way to Live a Truly Blessed Life

EAGLE KIM

RESOURCE *Publications* • Eugene, Oregon

THE MYSTERY OF CHRIST
The Way to Live a Truly Blessed Life

Resource Publications
An Imprint of Wipf and Stock Publishers
199 W. 8th Ave., Suite 3
Eugene, OR 97401

www.wipfandstock.com

PAPERBACK ISBN: 978-1-6667-5559-6
HARDCOVER ISBN: 978-1-6667-5560-2
EBOOK ISBN: 978-1-6667-5561-9

SEPTEMBER 21, 2022 1:05 PM

"He who eats My flesh and drinks My blood abides in Me, and I in him. As the living Father sent Me, and I live because of the Father, so he who eats Me, he also will live because of Me. "This is the bread which came down out of heaven; not as the fathers ate and died; he who eats this bread will live forever.""

JOHN 6:56–58

"This cup which is poured out for you is the new covenant in My blood."

LUKE 22:20

"Devote yourselves to prayer, keeping alert in it with an attitude of thanksgiving; praying at the same time for us as well, that God will open up to us a door for the word, so that we may speak forth the mystery of Christ, for which I have also been imprisoned . . ."

GAL 4:2–3

CONTENTS

....

PREFACE

....

Desire realized is sweet to the soul

(Prov 13:19)

Do you want to live a tranquil and successful life? The Bible guarantees that God will not only listen to our prayers, but will give us a blessed life. With the grace of God, we believe that everything will be okay. However, in life we experience many adversities, such as accidents, cancer, losing a job, or fear of the pandemic. Why must we suffer even if we trust in our loving God and believe in Him? What about Jesus' teaching, how with faith you can move mountains into the sea (Mark 11:23)? Did He say this simply as meaningless encouragement? When accidents happen to believers, and if God is there, why doesn't God protect His children who believe in the Almighty God? Those misunderstandings actually come from misinterpretation of the faith. In this book, I will explain what Biblical faith is, and how it works in your daily life. Perhaps some of your questions about why calamities happen will be answered.

I will also cover the suffering of Job. Do you believe that God gave Satan permission to attack the innocent believer Job in order to test Job's faith and eventually bless him later? Surprisingly, many people do. There are not many satisfactory answers as to why such horrible tragedies happened to Job. What kind of God would play a game with Satan, resulting in the suffering of His honest servant?

What kind of God makes a deal with Satan, the paragon of evil? What kind of Almighty God does not prevent awful catastrophes, but watches them in His comfort? It does not make any sense; however, these questions come from the assumption that Job was forever a good man. In the name of their own tradition and theological knowledge, many people misunderstand God's love for Job and insist that their interpretation is correct. Due to this insistence and stubbornness, many believers are hopeless beings living lonely and turbulent lives. I will explain not only why Job suffered such a terrible disaster, but also how you can prevent such misfortune.

I will show you the way to turn all of your problems into solutions, to prevent disasters, and to live a glorious life as the Lord promises in the Bible. Whenever people are met with distress, they complain and consider it bad luck, or try to find a source to blame. However, the Scripture tells us that the will of God is to rejoice always and give thanks in every circumstance. How do you live like this? The answer lies ahead. Your life can change. Your problems will not sidetrack your life anymore. I sincerely request that when you read this book, you put aside all your disputes and have faith in me as we move forward. The biblical quotations are from the *New American Standard Bible* (NASB) (Foundation Publication, 1995).

LIST OF ABBREVIATIONS

....

Old Testament	Abbreviation
Genesis	Gen
Exodus	Exod
Leviticus	Lev
Numbers	Num
Deuteronomy	Deut
Joshua	Josh
Judges	Judg
Ruth	Ruth
1 Samuel	1 Sam
2 Samuel	2 Sam
1 Kings	1 Kgs
2 Kings	2 Kgs
1 Chronicles	1 Chr
2 Chronicles	2 Chr
Ezra	Ezra
Nehemiah	Neh
Esther	Esth
Job	Job
Psalm	Ps

Proverbs	Prov
Ecclesiastes	Eccl
Song of Solomon	Song
Isaiah	Isa
Jeremiah	Jer
Lamentations	Lam
Ezekiel	Ezek
Daniel	Dan
Hosea	Hos
Joel	Joel
Amos	Amos
Obadiah	Obad
Jonah	Jon
Micah	Mic
Nahum	Nah
Habakkuk	Hab
Zephaniah	Zech
Malachi	Mal

New Testament	**Abbreviation**
Matthew	Matt
Mark	Mark
Luke	Luke
John	John
Acts	Acts
Romans	Rom
1 Corinthians	1 Cor
2 Corinthians	2 Cor
Galatians	Gal

List of Abbreviations

Ephesians	Eph
Philippians	Phil
Colossians	Col
1 Thessalonians	1 Thess
2 Thessalonians	2 Thess
1 Timothy	1 Tim
2 Timothy	2 Tim
Titus	Titus
Philemon	Phlm
Hebrews	Heb
James	Jas
1 Peter	1 Pet
2 Peter	2 Pet
1 John	1 John
2 John	2 John
3 John	3 John
Jude	Jude
Revelation	Rev

CHAPTER *1*

BLESSED LIFE

•••

BE ANXIOUS FOR NOTHING?

D o you recall a famous verse, "The Lord is my shepherd, I shall not want. He makes me lie down in green pastures" (Ps 23:1–2)? In reality, you still are in want. The Scripture says in Philippians 4:6–7, "be anxious for nothing." You might protest, how can I not be anxious in this dire situation? When you are anxious or worried, others might say that after your most difficult times, you will look back and see them as the most blessed times. Your pastor may say that God Almighty watches over you and protects you from destruction. If you are not able to, you should pray. However, your issues do not simply go away. You may have a lot of anxieties, including financial and health problems. Even if they are currently alright, you may worry about your future. How do you overcome this? Why do those words in the Bible seem far away from reality in this world? Why are your prayers not answered?

When I was a young minister of a Korean church near Boston, Massachusetts, an elder's son in our church was dying from cancer. He was in his early forties. He had a wife and a teenage daughter. His mother prayed for him to heal every day, morning and night. I also visited him at the hospital to pray for him several times. Later on, he died in spite of our ceaseless prayer. I could not

1

find the right words to console his mother and family. His death was a blow to his elderly mother. It was unimaginable how great the widow and young girl's sorrow was. Later on, another church member also died of cancer, leaving behind his young wife. At the funeral, I delivered a sermon saying that we should trust God no matter what happens to us. However, I was so disappointed in God because He didn't listen to our prayers. I questioned myself, thinking, how could I explain to them why God did not listen to our prayers? Where was God in our suffering and sorrow?

After that, a terrible and shocking incident in my young ministry life occurred. One of our church members abandoned his newlywed wife without any notice. The shock was so huge, not only to her, but also to me, because she married him through my matchmaking. I was ashamed to see her. I wondered how this could happen to me, a promising and devoted pastor. The guilt I carried that I might have contributed to ruining someone's life made me restless. Her husband was what most would call a sincere and devoted deacon. Since he joined our church, he had been very faithful. He eagerly attended Bible study and enthusiastically served. When I heard the news that he left his home without a single word to his wife, I didn't think it would be long before he came back. My expectation that he would return to his family changed from anger and disappointment when I heard that he was seeing other women. The feeling of betrayal was overwhelming. How could a faithful believer and deacon do something like this? Why were believers' lives not much different from the lives of non-believers? I almost gave up my ministry in despair.

Long ago, I attended a world mission conference sponsored by the American Church of Christ in Memphis, Tennessee. At the invitation of a friend, I attended the conference. Missionaries who were sponsored by the American Church of Christ got together to report on their work. It was there that I met an American missionary couple stationed in China. They showed me a plane ticket and asked me if I remembered the Korean Airlines flight in 1983 that was shot down by a Russian jet. On the cover of the plane ticket that they showed me was the mark of the Korean flag confirming that it was the plane ticket for the very flight that was shot down. The couple lived because they had miraculously missed the flight. Because of this second chance at life, they decided to dedicate the rest of their lives to God's work. To this couple, it was a true blessing that they had missed that flight. All the passengers who got to the airport on time and boarded the flight lost their lives. What if they had changed their schedule or cancelled the flight? If they arrived late to the airport and missed that flight because of heavy traffic or a minor accident, they still would have been alive. Why did this tragic accident happen to them? Why did the people who missed the flight end up being saved while those who made it on time lost their lives? Is God in control, or was this a matter of chance? There were innocent children on the flight; why did they have to die? We could continue to ask such questions, but few can provide a satisfying answer. What is the will of God in suffering? People of faith believe that God is an Almighty, loving, and ever-lasting God. God knows and cares for all human beings. If all of this is true, how can God allow these things to happen?

There are many promises in this Bible, and many churchgoers who read the Bible, but not everyone receives these promises. The Bible says that you will prosper, but people do not prosper and instead complain. The Bible says that you will be protected from evil, but people fall upon destruction and die all the time. Because these promises are not relevant to people's daily lives, when people are faced with difficulties, they simply give up. They are only grateful when good things happen. Yes, people trust in the Lord, but why are these promises not theirs?

WHY DOES GOD ALLOW THESE THINGS TO HAPPEN?

"Shock." People all over the world could not express it in more words. People wept in disbelief watching their televisions. This was America on Tuesday morning, September 11th, 2001. Shortly before 8 a.m. on 9/11, American Airlines Boeing 767, Flight 11, left Boston for Los Angeles. A hijacking happened shortly after takeoff.

Instead of heading to L.A., the plane, loaded with 92 people, turned to New York. It was 8:46 a.m. when the jet crashed into the 93rd through 98th floors of the World Trade Center's north tower. Then, sixteen and a half minutes later, United Airlines Flight 175, carrying 65 passengers, hit the south tower of the World Trade Center. The terror would not stop: a third hijacked jet slammed into the Pentagon. A fourth crashed in a Pennsylvania field, which was another hijacked plane that brave passengers thankfully prevented from causing more innocent deaths. Hundreds of passengers were killed. As the hours went by, the feeling of shock and horror had changed to sorrow and anger as people realized the enormous human loss and damage. Amid brave rescue missions, 343 firefighters lost their life. Here were a few of the comments made about the attack:

The fate of thousands inside the World Trade Center was sealed the moment the jets struck on Sept. 11. Nearly everyone below the crash zones lived, while only four people at or above the crash zones survived in the south tower. Compared to this, everyone on floors 92 and up were killed in the north tower, which was hit first. However, more than 1,000 people used the sixteen and a half minute gap between the first and second crash to safely evacuate the south tower's upper floors. It was reported that while everyone on the 92nd floor of the north tower was instantly killed when the airliners crashed into the building, everyone on the 91st floor amazingly survived. In each tower, 99 percent of the occupants below the crash survived. An analysis shows that two-thirds of the south tower occupants evacuated the upper floors during the sixteen and a half minutes between the attacks. In the north tower, an average of 78 people died per floor at the crash area and above, compared to 19 people per floor in the south tower. Before the collapsing of the towers, some people had time to phone, email or instant message farewells to loved ones watching on television. In an instant, many of victims lost their precious lives in the terrorist attacks, without keeping their promises to 'come back home soon.'

SO, WHERE IS GOD?

It is in times like these that many people claim bad luck, fate, or a mystery of life, to explain inexplicable circumstances. Prominent theologian Gabriel Fackre quoted, "Jesus wept. Tears rolled down the face of God at Ground Zero as surely as they did over Jerusalem." This is a reflection on Luke 19:41 as theological issues were raised by "the attack on America." Soon after 9/11, churches were packed with people, many of whom did not regularly attend worship service. They were seeking answers and comfort in the wake of the bloodiest day in recent American history. Priests and ministers across the country reflected on America's feelings of loss and grief, and they offered spiritual guidance over the weekend as millions attended church. Nearly every sermon touched on the topic, "where is God?" One pastor said, "People will ask, 'where was God on Tuesday, and how could a loving God allow this to happen?" His explanation: "hear me: God did not allow this to happen. It just happened. God was where God always is. He was there in the seat with every person who went down in the fiery furnace . . . God was there in the elevators and the stairwells of the World Trade Center." Another church minister could not explain this enormous disaster either. He claimed a similar explanation: "when the World Trade Center collapsed, God was there with them in the middle of fire, smoke, and rubble."

Do these kinds of sermons not bother you? God was there, but couldn't do anything? God was there to watch, but was powerless to do a single thing? It just happened? God remembers us and even numbers the very hairs of our heads. Luke 12:7 tells us, "Do not fear: you are of more value than many sparrows." Did God really helplessly observe this tragedy?

Where is God in tragedy or in our daily lives? How do we meet God and get help from God? God is in Christ. To meet God and to receive help from God, you must meet Christ first: "Now all these things are from God, who reconciled us to Himself through Christ and gave us the ministry of reconciliation, namely, that God was in Christ reconciling the world to Himself, not counting their trespasses against them, and He has committed to us the word of reconciliation" (2 Cor 5: 18–19). As a sinner, you cannot see God and have to reconcile with God through Christ, the mystery of Christ, by repenting your sins.

TRAGEDIES DON'T JUST HAPPEN

In Natick, Massachusetts, there was a rabbi by the name of Harold Kousner. He introduced himself as the rabbi that the members of his temple approach when they are facing problems and need counseling. This rabbi had a son who contracted the rare disease progeria, which causes rapid aging. The boy died in his early teens. This rabbi, after living through this tragedy, wrote a book titled, *When Bad Things Happen to Good People*. In his book, the rabbi rejects traditional reasons that tribulations are based in sin. Instead, he writes that bad things can and will happen to good people, and that in such cases even God cannot do everything because God is busy with more important things. He suggests that sometimes there is no reason for bad things to happen to good people, and that God leaves us room for human error.

He further explains that God cannot stop bad things from happening, but that He gives us the strength to overcome them and that is why one needs to believe in God. His theory is that even if one is not good, an innocent three-year-old must be good and if bad things happened to the child, then God must have limitations. The Bible verses he uses to support this are in the story of Job. In his own way, the rabbi defends God and yet denies the traditional doctrine of why people face misfortunes. In other words, he believes God is not a tyrant who waits to punish people every time they sin or make a mistake. However, according to the rabbi, He is a righteous God who has no choice but to stand by and watch as accidents happen. This rabbi's theory seems to make sense. Yet, traditional and conservative Christians believe that the cause for tragedy is sin, and they understand God as a very strict God who punishes sinners. Some Christians who have had their sins washed away and still face calamities believe that there is a hidden reason which people may not be aware of. Another potential cause may be that God tests us to increase our endurance and faith. In support of this, some Christians explain that God took away Job's children to bless him with even greater blessings. A different explanation is that because God loved Job's children so much, God took them up to Heaven early to spare them all the sicknesses and troubles that exist here on earth.

The thought of losing your own children, facing financial ruin, and going through horrendous trials and temptations, even as you maintain a strong faith in God as Job did, is not very comforting. If we adhere to this theory, then when one receives a lot of love from God, one should die early and go to Heaven sooner rather than stay here on earth and continue to face trials and tribulations. In other words, isn't it better to transfer quickly to the kingdom of God through a fatal accident? Following this logic, God would be a God who cannot do all things, which is what the rabbi professes.

Rather, God is a God who can only give us encouragement. It is for this reason that some people will support this kind of thinking in theology as new and enlightening. If one supposes, as this rabbi does, that God is not a God who can provide all solutions, then isn't it almost better not to rely on God whom you cannot see, and rely on parents, relatives and close friends instead? After all, these individuals are at your side and can provide you with tangible encouragement and compassion. A God who can only stand by passively and empathize when we face a problem is neither the God we want to believe in, nor the God Almighty, as the Bible professes.

If God is the Almighty and loving God, why then does God allow all kinds of tragedies? Does He in fact provide lessons to His children by giving and taking away life? Or is it a punishment caused by human sin? In Luke 13, there are two tragic stories. When Rome ruled over all Judea, Pilate used the Galileans' blood to mix with their sacrifices. Those who were killed for the Roman sacrifices must have been the "unlucky" ones. We do not know how many innocent people were killed like animals for sacrifices. The other story was one of a horrible accident. The tower in Siloam fell down and killed eighteen people. There was no modern equipment used to treat the injured. Some of them would have died instantly when the tower fell. Some of them survived the fall and died a slow and painful death from their injuries. The sorrow that the families of these victims is no different from any other time period. When Jesus heard of these tragic reports, He answered and said: "Now on the same occasion there were some present who reported to Him about the Galileans whose blood Pilate had mixed with their sacrifices. And Jesus said to them, "Do you suppose that these Galileans were greater sinners than all other Galileans because they suffered this fate? I tell you, no, but unless you repent, you will all likewise perish. Or do you suppose that those eighteen on whom the tower in Siloam fell and killed them were worse culprits than all the men who live in Jerusalem? "I tell you, no, but unless you repent, you will all likewise perish"" (Luke 13: 1–5).

Jesus is telling us not to judge other people's sins, but for us to continually repent. Without repentance, tragedies could happen to anyone. In other words, our repentance can prevent those unwanted horrible accidents. We do not know that those killed by accidents are greater sinners than us. Instead, we should repent frequently. 1 Samuel states: "The Lord kills and makes alive; He brings down to Sheol and raises up. The Lord makes poor and rich; He brings low, He also exalts. He raises the poor from the dust, He lifts the needy from the ash heap To make them sit with nobles, And inherit a seat of honor; For the pillars of the earth are the Lord's, And He set the world on them. He keeps the feet of His godly ones, But the wicked ones are silenced in darkness; For not by might shall a man prevail. Those who contend with the Lord will be shattered; Against them He will thunder in the heavens, The Lord will judge the ends of the earth; And He will give strength to His king, And will exalt the horn of His anointed" (1 Sam 2:6–10).

Why did these tragedies happen to those people? It happened because of their sins; however, we are not entitled to scrutinize others' sins, the sins of those that tragedies befall. Proverbs also mentions that the wicked are filled with misfortune, while the righteous do not have troubles. Some church pastors emphasize that the righteous will suffer. They believe that everyone who believes in God is righteous, popularly quoting Job. However, Job has quite a different interpretation. It is your choice whether to follow the Scripture or to support these churches' teaching. In short, all you can do is repent in order to prevent misfortunes.

Therefore, it is God who allows misfortunes, tragedies, and accidents. However, there must be a reason God permits such unwanted things. Have you noticed that the people who were destroyed in the wilderness were actually a baptized congregation? "And all were baptized into Moses in the cloud and in the sea" (1 Cor 10:2). Indeed, the Scripture tells us that they were part of the congregation in the church of the wilderness (Acts 7:37). They ate spiritual food and drank the spiritual drink from Christ. Nevertheless, they were killed and it was written for us as a warning, calling us to repent. Even though our fathers who were destroyed in the wilderness were all believers, they could not survive because of their sins: idolatry, immorality, and grumbling.

According to Galatians 5:24, you should crucify your flesh with passions and desire if you belong to Christ Jesus. However, so many believers actually fail to crucify their flesh. How do you crucify your earthly body so that it is dead to sins like passions and desire? Do you need to meditate in order to remove those sins every day as the monks of Zen Buddhism do? Of course not. What we need to do is repent those sins with the precious blood of Christ. Unfortunately, some church members still believe that attending worship service, participating in Bible study, and being involved church activities is sufficient to be a good Christian, and that eventually they will be sanctified without repentance. Some people even claim that we do not need to repent since we became children of God and are already saved.

Even if you profess to know God, your deeds are not acceptable to God, and your belief in Him will be detestable to God, as Titus proclaims,

They profess to know God, but by their deeds they deny
Him, being detestable and disobedient and worthless for
any good deed. (Titus 1:16)

That is why the first message of Jesus in his public life was
to repent and believe in the gospel, as Mark 1:15 also states, "The
time is fulfilled, and the kingdom of God is at hand; repent and
believe in the gospel." As we see here, Jesus' message is not to study
the gospel and then repent. In other words, you cannot believe in
the gospel without repentance. You may read and study the gospel
like a novel or history book. However, studying the gospel without
repentance does not make it spiritual food. Jesus also said, "But He
answered and said, "It is written, 'MAN SHALL NOT LIVE ON
BREAD ALONE, BUT ON EVERY WORD THAT PROCEEDS
OUT OF THE MOUTH OF GOD''" (Matt 4:4).

Sadly, many churches are eager to teach or emphasize that
Christians must study the gospel, but they do not teach repentance. Many believers are not aware of the mystery of Christ which
the apostle Paul preached (Col 4:3). As Jesus warned everybody,
the way to prevent disasters is to repent all sins. Whenever we hear
or see any calamities, we as believers and followers of Jesus Christ
should repent our sins. Unfortunately, most believers do not know
how important this is. At most, churchgoers try to comfort suffering people. As important as it is to console our neighbors, there
must also be humility and repentance. There is only one true
gospel which the apostles of Jesus and the apostle Paul preached.
However, people called by the grace of Christ abandon the gospel
and follow a different gospel (Gal 1:6–7).

THE ENDURANCE OF JOB

There is no question that we all want to live happily and comfort-
ably. However, sometimes instead of receiving the blessings and
happiness we desire, we are busy dealing with so many of life's
problems. They seem to appear in our lives continually and without warning. At the same time, many people believe that God

should simply provide the solutions to all of these problems. Some people feel that they surely know God and know Him well. But the problems in their lives do not seem to go away and they themselves admit to be in tribulations they do not desire to be in. Even those we call "good Christians" seem like they cannot escape the obvious misfortunes in their lives. Therefore, they believe that God allows life's problems to happen to good believers without any specific reason to test their faith. We cannot fully comprehend God Almighty and another human being's suffering, but through the Bible we can learn about God's personality and righteousness with the story of Job.

In the Old Testament, there was a man named Job who lived in the land of Uz. He was an untarnished, honest, and pious man. One day, Satan wanted to challenge Job's faith and got permission from God to ruin Job's wealth and physical health. Without any warning, nearly everything was taken from Job. He lost his sons and daughters by a great wind that struck his children's house, which fell and killed them. He lost his own house by the fire of God. Robbers then attacked Job and took his oxen and camels and killed all his servants. Nevertheless, Job didn't blame God. On the contrary, Job tore his robe, shaved his head, fell to the ground and worshiped Him. Job overcame his adversity without blaming God. Then, Satan suggested that Job's body be stricken. God once again allowed whatever Satan wanted, with the exception of killing Job. His body was afflicted with boils. Job had to use sharp materials to scrape the seepage from the sores and boils that covered his body. His wife cursed him and told him to "curse God and die." Then Job's three remaining friends heard all of this and visited him. They emphasized that the "innocent do not suffer and God is just." Job insisted his righteousness and integrity to his friends. When Job did not admit that he was not pure and innocent, Job's friends rebuked him. Job believed that God shattered him without any reason. Another friend of Job's claimed to speak for God and vindicated God's justice. Finally, God himself spoke to Job. Job's response was, "what can I say?" God showed His power. Job finally confessed and repented "in dust and ashes." God was pleased with

Job but not with Job's friends. However, when Job prayed for his friends, God forgave their sins. Finally, God restored Job's fortune and gave him new children.

There are many profound meanings and lessons in this famous Biblical story. James 5:11 tells us what the story of Job is all about—endurance: "Behold, we count those blessed who endured. You have heard of the endurance of Job and have seen the outcome of the Lord's dealings, that the Lord is full of compassion and is merciful." It is true that there would not have been a happy ending for Job without endurance. According to the Bible, endurance is essential in order to receive what God has promised us. Hebrew tells,

> Therefore, do not throw away your confidence, which has a great reward. For you have need of endurance, so that when you have done the will of God, you may receive what was promised. (Heb 10:35–36)

To receive what God promises, you need endurance. However, when a troubled life overpowers someone, it is not easy to ask them to have patience. Many people end their own lives, break off marriages, use drugs, etc. What we need to know is how ordinary people can have the patience that Job had. We should also note exactly why Job had such misfortunes.

It makes little sense, but answers originate from the idea that Job was always a good man. Ask yourself, if Job was such a righteous man before those ordeals, why did he need to repent later? The answer: "I have heard of You by the hearing of the ear; But now my eye sees You; Therefore I retract, And I repent in dust and ashes" (Job 42:5–6).

Clearly, Job had lost his righteousness. Other evidence for this is that he was under the power of Satan, as the Bible states, "And Satan answered the Lord and said, 'Skin for skin! Yes, all that a man has he will give for his life. However, put forth Thy hand, now, and touch his bone and his flesh; he will curse Thee to Thy face.' So the Lord said to Satan, 'Behold, he is in your power, only spare his life'" (Job 2: 4–6). Some may say that God actually gave Satan power, which is true because Satan cannot do anything without the permission of God Almighty. Ephesians states that Satan, the prince of the power of the air, is working in the sons of disobedience,

> And you were dead in your trespasses and sins, in which you formerly walked according to the course of this world, according to the prince of the power of the air, of the spirit that is now working in the sons of disobedience. (Eph 2:1–2)

Also, Ecclesiastes 7:20 states that "Indeed, there is not a righteous man on earth who continually does good and who never sins." As we see in the Scripture, there cannot be a man who is righteous forever. God does not have any partnership with Satan. The righteous God, the one true Judge, uses Satan as His tool to accomplish His goals. He is the most important reason why Job faced trials, because Job did not entirely trust Him. Note Job 3:25–26: "For what I fear comes upon me, And what I dread befalls me. I am not at ease, nor am I quiet, And I am not at rest, but turmoil comes."

Job actually lived in fear and anxiety, even as he had lived in comfort and wealth. From the outside, his life looked wonderful: plenty of cattle, many servants, and healthy sons and daughters. He also worshiped God diligently. Nevertheless, he had anxiety and fretfulness within his mind regarding his children. His ultimate fear was that God might have struck his sons and daughters due to their prodigality. While aging, his apprehension also might have grown, even though he prayed and worshiped God every day. Then, as Job confessed, his ultimate dread and fear became reality. Living in fear and anxiety is against the will of God. So, although Job was righteous, due to his restlessness he could not trust in God. 1 Peter warns: "casting all your anxiety on Him, because He cares for you. Be of sober spirit, be on the alert. Your adversary, the Devil, prowls around like a roaring lion, seeking someone to devour" (1 Pet 5:7–8).

The Devil is constantly looking for opportunity (Eph 5:27). How can we be on the alert to avoid his attacks? The answer is thanksgiving: "devote yourselves to prayer, keeping alert in it with attitude of thanksgiving" (Col 4:2).

To prevent providing the Devil with opportunity, we give thanks in everything, which is God's will for us in Christ Jesus (1 Thess 5:18). Proverbs also states that "what the wicked fears will come upon him, and the desire of righteous will be granted" (Prov 10:24).

There are more than 300 verses in the Bible regarding worry. For example, Matthew commands,

> Do not worry then, saying, 'What will we eat?' or 'What will we drink?' or 'What will we wear for clothing?' For the Gentiles eagerly seek all these things; for your heavenly Father knows that you need all these things. But seek first His kingdom and His righteousness, and all these things will be added to you. So do not worry about tomorrow; for tomorrow will care for itself. Each day has enough trouble of its own. (Matt 6:31–34)

Isaiah 41:10 reiterates, "'Do not fear, for I am with you; Do not anxiously look about you, for I am your God. I will strengthen you, surely I will help you, Surely I will uphold you with My righteous right hand.'" Thus, what we should fear is the Lord Almighty, not anything in this world, especially any human or catastrophe. Furthermore, Luke says:

> But I will warn you whom to fear: fear the One who, after He has killed, has authority to cast into hell; yes, I tell you, fear Him! Are not five sparrows sold for two cents? Yet not one of them is forgotten before God. Indeed, the very hairs of your head are all numbered. Do not fear; you are more valuable than many sparrows. (Luke 12: 5–7)

God's command is not to fear and to be anxious for nothing (Phil 4:6). To live in fear means that you disobey the command of God, and your future will be filled with the fruit of that fear you sow, just like Job's. Once again, the misunderstanding and misinterpretation of Job's story stems entirely from the definition of living in righteousness and faith. When Job's friends spoke of the wicked and how the triumph of the wicked is short, Job felt insulted and disputed their condemnation. However, when Jesus was despised and mocked by the people, He prayed for them to forgive their sins: "But Jesus was saying, "Father, forgive them; for they do not know what they are doing." And they cast lots, dividing up His garments among themselves. And the people stood by, looking on. And even the rulers were sneering at Him, saying, "He saved others; let Him save Himself if this is the Christ of God, His Chosen One." The soldiers also mocked Him, coming up to Him, offering Him sour wine, and saying, "If You are the King of the Jews, save Yourself!" Now there was also an inscription above Him, "THIS IS THE KING OF THE JEWS"" (Luke 23: 34–38).

Compared to Jesus, Job was very far from righteous. Faith actually means that Jesus Christ is in you (2 Cor. 13:5). Thus, if you have faith, you pray for those who insult you, unlike Job's actions toward his friends. Perhaps you have also heard the story of the Pharisee in Luke 18:

> And He also told this parable to some people who trusted in themselves that they were righteous, and viewed others with contempt: "Two men went up into the temple to pray, one a Pharisee and the other a tax collector. The Pharisee stood and was praying this to himself: 'God, I thank You that I am not like other people: swindlers, unjust, adulterers, or even like this tax collector. 'I fast twice a week; I pay tithes of all that I get.' But the tax collector, standing some distance away, was even unwilling to lift up his eyes to heaven, but was beating his breast, saying, 'God, be merciful to me, the sinner!' "I tell you, this man went to his house justified rather than the other; for everyone who exalts himself will be humbled, but he who humbles himself will be exalted. (Luke 18:9–14)

The Pharisees were so proud of their acts, and that they were unlike other sinners such as swindlers, the unjust, adulterers, or the tax collector. They were so diligent to practice fasting, praying and offering tithes. However, even though they justified their righteousness, Jesus considered them hypocrites. As you can see, what you believe or what you do will not make you justified, although being called unjustified even after you pray, give thanks, fast, and pay tithes would be alarming. When Jesus came to teach to the world, he censured the Pharisees in particular, who claimed to know the Scripture very well. The Pharisees were the most religious group at that time, yet Jesus perceived them to be hypocrites and a brood of vipers. The Pharisees considered themselves righteous and were proud of themselves, yet did not recognize they were sinners before God. Job's three friends judged him, just as the Pharisees judged others. God will judge who is righteous and who is not. Though many complain that life is not fair, the justice of God will rule and prevail over human life.

Galatians 3:3 clearly warns that someone could end up living by the flesh even if they begin by the Spirit. Even though Job was a man of God, he did not trust the Lord entirely, worrying about his child and living in fear. When you are double-minded, you become restless. Too many thoughts will interrupt your daily life and disrupt sleep. Even though Job's misfortune turned out well, what God wants for you is endurance without suffering. As 2 Thessalonians states, there is a way to live a peaceful and joyful life with the steadfastness of Christ and the love of God, which is the mystery of Christ.

> May the Lord direct your hearts into the love of God and
> into the steadfastness of Christ. (2 Thess 3:5)

CHAPTER 2

PRECIOUS BLOOD OF CHRIST

··

BE A BLESSED PERSON

C AN you define what a blessed person is? You may say that a blessed person is someone who has happiness, peace, health, and financial security. If you are prospering in all aspects and are in good health, just as your soul prospers, your life will be perfect (3 John 1:2). Some people have good health but no money, and some have money but their health is failing. Even if your life is successful in this world, if your soul is not saved, you will meet a tragic ending. As your soul prospers, your life should prosper and you should be healthy. These three things must go together.

The Bible guarantees that God will not only listen to our prayers, but will give us a prosperous life. According to Psalms, there is a way to be a blessed person.

> How blessed is the man who does not walk in the counsel of the wicked, Nor stand in the path of sinners, Nor sit in the seat of scoffers! But his delight is in the law of the Lord, And in His law he meditates day and night. He will be like a tree firmly planted by streams of water, Which

yields its fruit in its season And its leaf does not wither;
And in whatever he does, he prospers. (Ps 1:1–3)

Sadly, many church goers treat the Psalms as old fables or outdated lyrics. However, the Psalms are the words of the living God. There are two types of people in the first chapter of Psalms: the blessed and the wicked. If you trust the word of God and follow His word closely, you too can live a prosperous life. To live a prosperous life, according to Psalms, you should meditate on the Law day and night. In the Bible, there are two different conceptual words: the Law and the word of God. The Law, which was added in order to show what our sins are (Gal 3:19), gives us knowledge of sin, as stated, "Through the Law comes the knowledge of sin" (Rom 3:20).

Proverbs warns that if you do not listen to the Law, your prayer will become a thing of hatred to God: "He who turns away his ear from listening to the Law, Even his prayer is an abomination" (Prov 28:9).

The prayer you say every day can be detestable to God, unless you realize your sins through the Law. The church should be a house of prayer where church members realize their sins through the pastor's sermon, then repent those sins and pray for others. Praying for other people is our task in order to lead a quiet and peaceful life in our community (1 Tim 2:1–4).

Some Pharisees criticized Jesus and His disciples for transgressing the tradition of elders, which was to wash hands before eating bread. Jesus, in turn, taught that the things coming out of the mouth defiles man, rather than eating without washing hands. Matthew states that sins coming from the heart defile people:

> Do you not understand that everything that goes into the mouth passes into the stomach, and is eliminated? But the things that proceed out of the mouth come from the heart, and those defile the man. For out of the heart come evil thoughts, murders, adulteries, fornications, thefts, false witness, slanders. "These are the things which defile the man; but to eat with unwashed hands does not defile the man. (Matt 15:17–20)

Unfortunately, most churches ignore Jesus' teaching regarding sins from people's hearts. Have you considered why so many people live for money, even if they claim to be Christian? Evil thoughts are the equivalent of loving money (1 Tim. 6:10). Even after firmly deciding to live for God, your decision will not last, because the love of money is sin coming out of your heart. Have you ever felt guilty after looking at a woman with lust? You have already committed adultery with her in your heart. Even after deciding not to do it, you will do it again and again due to the sins of adultery and fornication coming from the heart. Even if you never killed anyone before, when you hate your brother, you are a murderer, according to 1 John 3:15. These sins come out of our hearts every day without our realizing it. If you clean these sins with the blood of Christ, your life will convert from an ordinary one to a blessed one, from a meaningless life to one giving glory to the Lord. Jesus hinted to His disciples that there was a more significant task than washing hands before eating bread. His disciples did not understand what He meant. Even today, after reading His explanation on what actually defiles men, many people do not pay attention to the sins coming from the heart.

Those sins defile you. If you do not clean them, you are a slave. The Apostle Paul commands in Romans 6:12, "Do not let sin reign in your mortal body so that you obey its lusts." Do you know how to not let sin reign in your mortal body? Many Christians insist that "we are not under law but under grace" (Rom 6:15). While this is true, you are the slave of sin whenever you commit it, resulting in death:

> For sin shall not be master over you, for you are not under law but under grace. What then? Shall we sin because we are not under law but under grace? May it never be! Do you not know that when you present yourselves to someone as slaves for obedience, you are slaves of the one whom you obey, either of sin resulting in death, or of obedience resulting in righteousness? (Rom 6:14–16)

Because of the sins that come from the heart, people become slaves of sin. They do not give thanks because of sins built up every day. But if you meditate on the Law day and night, you will prosper just as God promised and you will not be a slave of sin. It is clear that if your heart condemns you, you will lose your confidence before God and lose your prosperity (Heb 10:35–36).

God promises you will receive whatever you ask if your heart does not condemn you (1 John 3:21–22). What a wonderful promise this is! In order to maintain your confidence before God, you need to meditate on the Law day and night by realizing your sins through the Bible. 1 John also shows that God hears us in whatever we ask:

> This is the confidence which we have before Him, that, if we ask anything according to His will, He hears us. And if we know that He hears us in whatever we ask, we know that we have the requests which we have asked from Him. (1 John 5:14–15)

If you start to meditate on the Law of the Lord by realizing your sins through Scripture, your life will be completely different. Your prayers will be heard. Your heart will be filled with peace instead of fear and anxiety. Sin is a very powerful enemy. Sincere Christians acknowledge they are sinners but do not know what to repent, how to have their prayers answered, or how to change their lives. When you start to meditate on the Law, you will feel grateful in the hands of the Lord, and when you wash the sins that come from your heart and flesh, your life will never be the same. You bathe or shower every day because your body gets dirty. In the same way, you should repent. If you wash your sins away, you become confident so that you can ask anything according to His will, which is thanksgiving. If you ask with thanksgiving, God can fulfill your requests.

GOD'S WILL FOR YOU

Nobody looks forward to facing trials and tribulations. When problems arise, the quality of our lives begins to deteriorate. We then become preoccupied with those problems. Who doesn't want to live a joyful and blessed life? This principle is simple: if you sow joy and happiness, you will eat the fruit of bliss and contentment. This is the promise of God, not a man-made theory. The issue is how to daily plant or "sow" the life we expect to receive. We often live in stress, sometimes leading to anger or depression. Because of these negative emotions, we end up hating or judging others. If you live with anger, hate, or judgment, you are planting seeds. For example, if you plant the seed of anger, you will reap the fruit of anger in return. Building upon the example of anger, it is our job to contain that anger or other negative emotions within our own thoughts, without outbursts. Some people explode when they get angry or emotional. In your heart you know that such explosive action is not right, and you may experience regret from your actions.

Whenever you encounter this situation, you automatically—impulsively—explode again and again. You might defend yourself, claiming "that person deceived me, cheated me, betrayed me, was violent toward me, and is my enemy," or "how can you say it is my fault?" In the end, it is your fault. Even though you may not bear in mind what you have done, the righteous God remembers all your deeds, words, and even thoughts. God keeps this record for ultimate judgment. Yet, before God ever judges anyone, they will have a chance to repent. Moreover, most people do not remember that all their thoughts and actions will one day be judged. Many simply continue to blame and hate, and end up committing sin carelessly. These problems are then compounded as seeds of negative emotions yielding fruit and God's judgment. 1 Thessalonians plainly show us the rule of the righteous God:

> This is a plain indication of God's righteous judgment so that you may be considered worthy of the kingdom of God, for which indeed you are suffering. For after all it is only just for God to repay with affliction those who afflict you, and to give relief to you who are afflicted and to us as well when the Lord Jesus shall be revealed from heaven with His mighty angels in flaming fire, dealing out retribution to those who do not know God and to those who do not obey the gospel of our Lord Jesus. And

these will pay the penalty of eternal destruction, away from the presence of the Lord and from the glory of His power, (1 Thess 1: 5–9)

By misunderstanding the rule of God, we expend all sorts of effort, but rather than finding solutions, we mostly end up frustrated as we try to root out the bad fruit we are reaping. We are continually faced with problems, big and small, and do not see any solutions to them. Many end up defeated, claiming that life is unfair. Some people even go as far as taking their own lives or committing crime because they are hopeless.

Do you know what God's will is for you? Not long ago, I read a book by one of the most prominent preachers and writers in the U.S. Throughout the book, I could clearly see that he was a sincere believer. However, according to him, God's will for us as human beings is "mysterious and unpredictable." I respectfully disagree. In the Bible, God plainly tells us His will: "Rejoice always; pray without ceasing; in everything give thanks; for this is God's will for you in Christ Jesus" (1 Thess 5:16–18).

"Rejoice always," and "give thanks in everything"? Believe it or not, this is God's will for us. Perhaps you are wondering if the Apostle Paul recorded this not knowing how complex life would become in the years to come. Whether or not he did, God knows the future. God's will for us is to live a life filled with joy, thanksgiving, and peace. Because we have to sow joy and thanksgiving in order to live joyfully, this is the will of God for you and me by default. Always does not mean sometimes. Always is not concerned with how we feel either. Always means every day and all the time, whether we experience emotional joy or not.

How can we do this? How can we give thanks during tragic moments? It sounds inconceivable and impossible. But is it really? Why would God ask us to do something we cannot do? Why is giving thanks in all circumstances God's will for us? Because dilemmas in our life arise from what we have done in the past, the loving God always gives us a chance to repent throughout our lives. Without repentance of our sins, we are slaves of sin and of the Devil, and do not belong to God. John tells us that we will have life: "Jesus therefore said to them again, 'Truly, truly, I say to you, I am the door of the sheep. All who came before Me are thieves and robbers, but the sheep did not hear them. I am the door; if anyone enters through Me, he shall be saved, and shall go in and out, and find pasture. The thief comes only to steal, and kill, and destroy; I came that they might have life, and might have it abundantly" (John 10:7–10).

It is clear that we will reap what we sow. How then can we remember and repent what we have done in the past? Today's life is directly related to the life you lived yesterday. To correct what we have done in the past, we must "pray without ceasing," meaning we must repent. Whenever you repent your sins, God will turn your life of misery into a blessed life, as stated in Psalms:

> You have turned for me my mourning into dancing; You have loosed my sackcloth and girded me with gladness, That my soul may sing praise to You and not be silent. O Lord my God, I will give thanks to You forever. (Ps 30:11–12)

Most Christians know how important prayer is, and that prayer is the key element to receiving the promise of God. Conversely, most people do not know that God does not hear your prayer when you have sins: "If I regard wickedness in my heart, The Lord will not hear;" (Ps 66:18). Isaiah also tells that:

> Behold, the Lord's hand is not so short That it cannot save; Nor is His ear so dull That it cannot hear. But your iniquities have made a separation between you and your God, And your sins have hidden His face from you so that He does not hear. (Isa 59:1–2)

The many tragedies that you see, hear, and experience are to remind you of previous sins. If you live with this principle, you can pray without ceasing. Those instances provide an opportunity to clean your heart. Without such opportunities, we would forget our sins. All accidents are a mirror to remind you of your sins, which call for repentance. If you live with this principle, then you can give thanks in all circumstances. For example, if somebody insults you, God is showing you what you sowed before and giving you the chance to repent and to be clean. Therefore, you can easily offer thanks to Him. Moreover, there is no reason to fight with that person, since it is for your own good. Now you can sow thanksgiving instead of anger. Your life can then improve greatly. Your life will also be filled with thanks and blessings from God. That is why Jesus tells us that the church should be "a house of prayer" (Luke 19:46). In other words, the church should be a place that converts problems and sins in our life into the will of God through repentance.

A church should be a very busy place, filled with repentance and intercessory prayer for others. Sadly, many churches are too busy with other activities and entertainment. Even though church members are suffering, pastors will try to comfort them or encourage them, instead of giving them the answer to their problems: repentance. In their sermons, most pastors emphasize prayer, yet do not repent. Most church goers also know that worship is a key element of church. Worship is important; however, according to Ecclesiastes 5:1, listening to the word of God is more important than worshipping, as stated: "Guard your steps as you go to the house of God and draw near to listen rather than to offer the sacrifice of fools; for they do not know they are doing evil" (Eccl 5:1).

Why is listening to the word of God so important? The word of God as the Law makes you aware of your sins, which you may have forgotten. In addition, listening to the word of God is important in following the will of God. A sermon of worship should be able to awaken hidden sins of the church members, as Ecclesiastes confirms, "The words of wise men are like goads, and masters of these collections are like well-driven nails; they are given by one Shepherd" (Eccl 12:11).

Therefore, the role of the sermon is to reveal the congregation's sins as well as give encouragement to follow the word of God.

When I was thirteen years old, I started attending church regularly. The church wasn't too far from downtown Seoul, and our congregation consisted of three-hundred people. At the time, several elders of the church were very wealthy people who owned their own companies. They used to give Sunday school students nice gifts on Christmas. However, their companies ended up going out of business. One elder was in so much debt that he was arrested and couldn't come to church.

My friends called him elder Job, after Job in the Bible. Many misfortunes happened to members of my church. One of the deacons' factories burned down. On his way home from an early morning service, one of the elders was hit by a car and died. Even my pastor's young son died from cancer when he was just fifteen years old. The pastor could not teach about blessings. He emphasized that believers' anguish and misery came from God. During Bible study, our group used to discuss why God allowed such unwanted agony to the church members. As a young, novice believer, I could not participate in these discussions, but I listened.

When I become a high school student, I was traumatized by my mother's sickness, cirrhosis of the liver. According to the doctor's diagnosis, my mother would not live through the year. My father was an executive manager of the office of Korean National Railroads. Even though he was too busy for me, he emphasized the importance of receiving a good education. I had to study very hard to enter an excellent high school and college in order to please my parents. It was common to study from five o'clock in the morning to eleven at night. The only thing I ever had in mind was entering the best university. In spite of this, adding to the stress of my mother's illness, my father was hit by a car and hospitalized for more than two months. All day long at school, my thoughts dwelled on the apprehension of my mother and father's deaths. After school, I spent most of my nights with my father at the hospital and couldn't study. Going to school unprepared each day was agony. Along with feeling empty and devastated, I was so afraid of being behind in my academic achievement. Life seemed so uncertain to me. I was lonely and desperate, so I started to look for something to comfort me. Even though I had attended church for more than six years, I did not know that I had to repent my sins. There was nothing left to do except pray. Church was the only place I could escape from my anger and worries. Outwardly, I became a sincere Christian with strong faith. Still, I asked myself many times, why doesn't God listen to my prayers? As the Bible promises in Matthew 7:7–12, "Ask, and it shall be given to you; seek, and, and you shall find; knock, and it shall be opened to you." However, my church hardly mentioned repentance. What I learned instead was that I was already righteous, and that God would answer my prayer someday.

ESCAPING FROM THE SLAVERY OF SIN

There was a young man was named John. At a very early age, John became the priest of a local church. He was a committed and sincere man, devoted to the work of God. His congregation liked his humble and friendly demeanor. Soon he won public recognition and his church grew to become the largest church around. Many people in town respected him as a spiritual leader, and even politicians came to him for advice and spiritual guidance. One day, he was accused and later convicted of molesting children. He was sentenced to eight years in prison. What could have led to his downfall? How could a devoted believer become such a disgraceful and fallen man? This illustration mirrors many recent sex-abuse scandals that are coming out against Catholic priests. The archdiocese faces hundreds of lawsuits involving other priests and bishops. How is it possible that after more than 30 years of being devoted to God, a priest could be a sexual offender?

Once again, we as sinners do not have any right to condemn other people's acts. Jesus challenged us, "He who is without sin among you, let him be the first to throw a stone at her" (John 8:7). Yet, we should still know that devoted Christians can be false believers at any given time. According to John, no one can steal any followers away from the Almighty one's care: "My Father, who has given them to Me, is greater than all; and no one is able to snatch them out of the Father's hand" (John 10:29). If this is the case, how do believers lose their faith? It is true that no one cannot snatch you from God. However, you surely reject God because of your sins. Without repentance, your corrupt minds commit unrighteous acts, denying God with your behavior. There are sins coming from your heart which lead to a depraved mind:

> And just as they did not see fit to acknowledge God any longer, God gave them over to a depraved mind, to do those things which are not proper, being filled with all unrighteousness, wickedness, greed, evil; full of envy, murder, strife, deceit, malice; they are gossips, slanderers, haters of God, insolent, arrogant, boastful, inventors of evil, disobedient to parents, without understanding, untrustworthy, unloving, unmerciful; and although they know the ordinance of God, that those who practice such things are worthy of death, they not only do the same, but also give hearty approval to those who practice them. (Rom 1:28–32)

When you keep repenting the sins in your hearts with the blood of Christ, you will be in Christ and Christ will enter your hearts. Then, you are able to worship God with a purified mind.

When I was a seminarian, I had the chance to spend time with many Fathers and nuns for the Clinical Pastoral Education at a homeless shelter in the city. Some of the Fathers and nuns shared their guilt about having sexual urges whenever they saw an attractive woman or man. Because those Fathers and nuns gave up marriage, I mistakenly thought that they did not have any sextual desires. They asked me (the only married man in the group at the time) whether I had had the same feelings or not. Hearing their talk made me feel embarrassed. I was not used to talking about sex in public. However, I admit that I had committed the exact same sins over and over again, even after marriage. I know many sincere and dedicated Fathers and pastors, but I never asked them about guilt surrounding immorality. It seemed like there was no way to overcome this annoying sin and feelings of guilt. What is God's intent by mentioning adultery? If God warns us, there is always a way to overcome these sins. In the Scripture, there is a very powerful way to govern, which is to repent the sins coming from the flesh with the blood of Christ. By obeying the Bible, I have been able to overcome such a sin. Just as Jesus said, "the truth will make you free" (John 8:32). It is no wonder that we as human beings, pastors, Fathers and nuns could lust easily without repenting our sins. Jesus warns us in Matthew 5:28 that "everyone who looks at a woman with lust for her has already committed adultery with her in his heart."

Do not disregard this warning. If you have a lustful mind, you cannot go to Heaven, according to this and so many other verses. This applies to everybody, men and women alike. That being said, who is able to stay away from committing this sin? Am I completely free from committing adultery in my heart? The answer is yes and no. It is my testimony that whenever I repent those sins regularly, I absolutely do not have any such desire in my heart. However, if I stop repenting those sins, my mind suddenly becomes occupied with lust.

Regrettably, many church goers do not know how to escape from the slavery of sin. They argue that because we continually commit sins because of our sinful nature, no one can go to Heaven. So, when you believe in Jesus as your Savior, you are saved. However, this is not a teaching of the Scripture, but a man-made doctrine by church leaders who do not know how to prevent sin from reigning the body. The true Scripture's teaching is that when you commit sins, you are slaves of sin resulting in death. Instead of glorifying God with good works before other people (Matt 5:16), many church goers have insulted the name of God with their misdemeanors. The main reason is that they did not know how to prevent slavery to sin. In other words, they ignored the sins that defiled them.

The word of God will be accomplished without changing the smallest letter or stroke (Matt 5:18). Do not be fooled by the doctrine of men. The word indicates that when you are calling someone 'fool', it means you are already defiled by the sins coming from your heart. People do not realize that when you hate someone, you are a murderer according to 1 John 3:15. The Scripture has promised to give you freedom from all kinds of things: sins, disasters, worries, disease. If you repent sins with the blood of Christ (Eph 1:7), whenever you feel fear and unrest, your mind will be refreshed. The blood of Christ is a powerful, precious, and priceless gift from the Lord. I have a plethora of testimonies for repentance, and I hope you will be one of them in the near future.

Long ago, I suffered from chronic asthma that developed from seasonal allergies. My family doctor tried to lessen my symptoms by using several different medicines before sending me to a specialist. I could hardly sleep at night because of a very severe cough, even after seeing an allergy specialist. He decided to prescribe oral steroids, but my overall symptoms did not improve.

After my symptoms worsened, I started to look for anything to diminish my asthma. I attended several famous televangelist revival meetings in hopes of being healed. From one meeting to the next, people kept coming forward claiming that they were completely healed. Yet, my asthma did not go away. On the contrary, I could hardly breathe and could not sleep without using inhalers. One famous evangelist, who claimed to have spiritual healing power from God, held his revival meeting only twice a year. I was so desperate that I went to England to attend his revival meeting. After singing praise songs for about an hour, the speaker finally started preaching about divine healing, and then invited anyone to be healed. After his prayer, people started saying how God touched them and healed their sickness, but again, I was not one of them. Nothing seemed to help me get better.

After I learned to repent the sins in Matthew 15:19, Romans 1:28–32, and Galatians 5:19–21, I started to repent these sins for several hours every night. I could not fall asleep anyway due to severe coughing. One night, while I was on a half-empty flight, I was able to lie down and fall asleep right after takeoff. During my sleep, I felt chilly and covered my body with a blanket that the airline provided. I was especially allergic to fur-like substances, but I slept soundly without trouble. After waking up, I realized that I shouldn't have used the blanket because of my condition. I was amazed that I did not have an asthma attack. Ever since, I have not suffered from asthma. I do not have to use a steroid inhaler and I no longer have seasonal allergy symptoms. I have witnessed so many wonderful things in my life and other people's lives after I began to share this Biblical wonder.

THE GOD OF THE LIVING

There was an ambitious man in the Old Testament. His name was Jacob, meaning "one who takes by the heel." Jacob and his twin brother Esau struggled with one another in even their mother's womb. Esau became firstborn over Jacob in their first fight. However, Jacob never gave up his goal to be the firstborn child, and decided to steal Esau's birthright. Esau returned from working in the field one day very hungry, and Jacob had cooked some stew. When Esau asked his brother to have some of the stew, Jacob insisted that Esau should sell his birthright to him. Esau accepted, as it would be a mistake to refuse while starving. However, after eating, Esau realized what he had done. That is why Genesis uses the somewhat harsh word, "despised," to describe his mistake instead of saying, "treated his birthright lightly." Genesis states, "Then Jacob gave Esau bread and lentil stew; and he ate and drank, and rose and went on his way. Thus Esau despised his birthright" (Gen 25:34).

Later on, Jacob tried to steal his father's blessing for Esau with the help of his mother Rebekah. Esau lost his chance to receive the blessing from his father as the firstborn. The one who ultimately received the blessing was Jacob and not Esau. Esau made his mind up to kill his brother rather than to repent. He did not comprehend that the true source of blessings is the Lord, not his father. He lived however he wanted without repenting his sins and brought grief to his family. Jacob, the blessed man, had to flee from Esau's wrath and became a servant of his uncle, Laban. Laban deceived Jacob in many ways. Compared to Jacob's life, Esau's seemed much more peaceful and affluent, even without the blessing from his father. The book of Hebrews testifies that he found no place for repentance though he sought for it with tears:

> See to it that no one comes short of the grace of God;
> that no root of bitterness springing up causes trouble,
> and by it many be defiled; that there be no immoral or

godless person like Esau, who sold his own birthright for a single meal. For you know that even afterwards, when he desired to inherit the blessing, he was rejected, for he found no place for repentance, though he sought for it with tears. (Heb 12:15–17)

These verses warn you that if you do not continue to repent your sins, in the end, you might not have the chance to repent like Esau. The Scripture tells us that Esau's sin is the same as immorality or ungodliness. If you do not repent sins of immorality or ungodliness, you will not inherit the kingdom of God:

> Now the deeds of the flesh are evident, which are: immorality, impurity, sensuality, idolatry, sorcery, enmities, strife, jealousy, outbursts of anger, disputes, dissensions, factions, envying, drunkenness, carousing, and things like these, of which I forewarn you, just as I have forewarned you, that those who practice such things will not inherit the kingdom of God. (Gal 5:19–21)

The Scripture forewarns us that we will not inherit the kingdom of God by practicing the sins mentioned in Galatians 5:19–21. Even with such a warning, many churches ignore these verses. Esau was not only rejected from inheriting the blessing, but also the kingdom of God, as indicated by Scripture. The book of Romans also informs that anyone who is according to the flesh sets their minds on the things of the flesh, and the result is death and hostility toward God. "For those who are according to the flesh set their minds on the things of the flesh, but those who are according to the Spirit, the things of the Spirit. For the mind set on the flesh is death, but the mind set on the Spirit is life and peace, because the mind set on the flesh is hostile toward God; for it does not subject itself to the law of God, for it is not even able to do so, and those who are in the flesh cannot please God" (Rom 8:5–8).

How do you overcome the flesh? You must repent those sins coming from your flesh. With those sins, you are dead and cannot please God. God is not the God of the dead. Esau's name did not belong to the living. Mark states:

> But regarding the fact that the dead rise, have you not read in the book of Moses, in the passage about the burning bush, how God spoke to him, saying, 'I am the God of Abraham, the God of Isaac, and the God of Jacob'? He is not the God of the dead, but of the living; you are greatly mistaken. (Mark 12:26–27)

Esau's grandfather was Abraham, who became a blessing (Gen 12:1–3). Esau's father, Isaac, was also a devoted person of God. So, Esau was born and raised knowing the Lord. Yet, he repeatedly picked his own fleshly desires over spiritual guidance. He represents godless men who choose immorality but claim to be believers. Recall the story of Exodus, when the Israelites left Egypt. The king of Egypt, Pharaoh, decided to pursue the Israelites after he freed them from slavery (Exod 14:1–31). When the Israelites arrived at the Red Sea, there was no escape from the Egyptian army. However, the Almighty God showed them mercy by dividing the sea. The Israelites were able to pass while the following army was destroyed in the midst the sea. The Apostle Paul reinterpreted this incident in Corinthians:

> For I do not want you to be unaware, brethren, that our fathers were all under the cloud and all passed through the sea; and all were baptized into Moses in the cloud and in the sea; and all ate the same spiritual food; and all drank the same spiritual drink, for they were drinking from a spiritual rock which followed them; and the rock was Christ. (1 Cor 10:1–4)

The Israelites who witnessed the powerful hand of God before their very eyes were a baptized congregation. They ate and drank the spiritual food. They experienced how the Almighty God protected them through miracles. However, they were denied entry to the Promised Land and perished in the wilderness. Unfortunately, today's churches do not warn their members about falling and losing their faith, even after they are baptized and witness God's mercy. 1 Corinthians tells why these verses are recorded: "Now these things happened as examples for us, that we should not crave evil thing, as they also craved" (1 Cor 10:6). 1 Corinthians also confirms,

> Now these things happened to them as an example, and they were written for our instruction, upon whom the ends of ages have come. (1 Cor 10:11)

Two major sins they engaged in were immorality and complaint. Immorality is the same sin Esau committed. Who can be free from these sins? Immorality is a sin from our flesh. It is too powerful to overcome simply by effort. We should not judge the Catholic priests who molested children. Their dedicated lives to God were shattered by immorality. In my opinion, those Fathers did not know how to overcome such immorality. I am not here to defend them either. But it is impossible to rule over sexual desire with one's own self-determination.

After spending twenty years under Laban's roof, Jacob's own household grew to the size of sixteen people: two wives, two maids, eleven sons, and himself (Gen 32:22). Soon realizing that he could not stay with Laban any longer, Jacob decided to go back to his hometown. By then, Jacob had become very successful, and could return in wealth and glory if he wished. However, Jacob still had an Achilles heel. Jacob was so afraid that Esau might kill him even though twenty years had passed, but decided to take the risk anyway. Jacob received news that Esau brought 400 men to meet his brother. That night, just before crossing the ford of the Jabok, Jacob was alone and wrestled with an angel. Jacob prevailed and received a blessing from the angel (Gen 32:24–32). The book of Hosea reinterpreted that story as follows:

> The Lord also has a dispute with Judah, And will punish Jacob according to his ways; He will repay him according to his deeds. In the womb he took his brother by the heel, And in his maturity he contended with God. Yes, he wrestled with the angel and prevailed; He wept and sought His favor. He found Him at Bethel And there He spoke with us, (Hos 12:2–4)

What the book Hosea tells us here is that Jacob was pun-
ished according to his ways. Laban's treachery against Jacob (Gen
29:15–35) and Esau's threatening to kill Jacob were a part of his
punishment from the Lord. After recognizing his sins, Jacob wept
and repented his sins in front of God. God does not despise a
broken and a contrite heart (Ps 51:17). God, whose name is Holy,
dwells with the contrite and lowly of spirit in order to revive the
spirit of the lowly and to revive the heart of the contrite (Isa 57:15).
After repenting at the Jabok during the night, Jacob became a completely different person. He went from being a coward to being
as bold as a lion (Prov 28:1). Before that night, Jacob planned to
stay behind his family in order to escape Esau's attack. After repentance, he came forward to meet his brother without any fear
and reconciled with Esau. After making peace with his brother,
Jacob's life seemed prosperous and devoid of troubles. Yet a big-
ger problem was still waiting for him and his whole household. In
accordance with Genesis 34, Dinah, Jacob's daughter, was forced
to lay with Shechem, the son of Hamor the Hivite. Jacob's sons
deceitfully accepted Hamor's intermarriage proposal between two
inhabitants. Simeon and Levi killed not only Hamor, his son, and
every male in the village but also looted all their wealth and took
all their children and wives. If their neighbors, the Canaanites and
the Perizzites decide to avenge Shechem, Jacob's household would
be destroyed. Jacob's fear was so great that it did not even compare
to his fear of Esau's revenge. Therefore, Jacob said to Simeon and
Levi, "You have brought troubled on me by making me odious
among the inhabitants of the land, among the Canaanites and the
Perizzites; and my men being few in number, they will gather together against me and attack me and I will be destroyed, I and my
household" (Gen 34:30). This incident would be the climax of everything Jacob had encountered during his unpleasant sojourning
(Gen 47:9). Its impact was so enormous that Jacob cursed Simeon
and Levi and left them no blessing before he died:

> Simeon and Levi are brothers; Their swords are imple-
> ments of violence. "Let my soul not enter into their
> council; Let not my glory be united with their assembly;

Because in their anger they slew men, And in their self-will they lamed oxen. "Cursed be their anger, for it is fierce; And their wrath, for it is cruel. I will disperse them in Jacob, And scatter them in Israel. (Gen 49: 5–7)

Still, Jacob's life was not ruined by all this. Jacob told his household and all who were with him to put away foreign gods and purify themselves. Then, Jacob remembered how God answered his prayer. Because of Jacob's quick determination to kneel down before God, no one pursued Jacob's household (Gen 35:5). Realize that the repentance of your sins is the key to escape from your distress. Some people say they worship God, not idols. However, If you have greed, it is the same as idolatry. If you do not repent these sins, God's wrath will come upon you as the Scripture indicates:

Therefore consider the members of your earthly body as dead to immorality, impurity, passion, evil desire, and greed, which amounts to idolatry. For it is because of these things that the wrath of God will come upon the sons of disobedience, (Col 3:5–6)

God's wrath will come upon those who disobey, because of the sins of immorality that amount to idolatry. Many churches have ignored repenting these crucial sins, making church members worse than secular persons. While Esau was trapped by his wrath, plotting to kill his own brother, Jacob commanded his people to put away foreign gods, indicating that we have to repent the greediness that brings the wrath of God unto our lives. Jacob also asked his household to purify themselves.

The only way to purify yourself is to clean your sins with the blood of Christ (Eph 1:7). Jacob's second command was to change garments, also pointing out that we must repent our sins. Conclusively, the way to receive forgiveness for our sins is to repent and to be baptized (Acts 2:38). Clothing yourself in Christ means you are baptized. Churches that do not practice repentance are not much different from nonbelievers, suffering from disasters, broken relationships, and disease.

YOUR PRAYERS WILL BE ANSWERED

No one can deny that prayer is one of the most important compo-
nents of spiritual life. There are so many promises in the Bible that
when you pray, your prayers will be answered. Many church goers
will keep the habit of praying whether those prayers are answered
or not. An interesting story occurs in the book of Mark. Jesus took
three of his beloved disciples, Peter, James, and John to a high
mountain. After witnessing Jesus' transfiguration on the mountain,
Peter suggested that they had better stay there and make three tab-
ernacles. However, Jesus brought them back to reality by showing
them sicknesses and all kinds of misfortunes. When Jesus and the
three disciples came back to join the rest of the disciples, a father
brought his demon-possessed son to Jesus. Before Jesus returned,
the disciples had a chance to heal the young boy. They had already
seen many times that Jesus was able to cast out unclean spirits. It
looked easy to do, and they felt pity for the boy. At any rate, they
failed to cast the demon out. The father begged Jesus to heal him.
The father said, "'if you can do anything, take pity on us and help
us!' And Jesus said to him, 'If You can? All things are possible to
him who believes'" (Mark 9:22).

Is this true? Can anything happen when you believe? Or did
this only happen during Jesus' time? Let's examine this story further. When Jesus replied to the boy's father, immediately the boy's
father cried out and said, 'I do believe; help my unbelief' (Mark
9:22–24). You can interpret this verse in many ways. When Jesus
says, "all things are possible to him who believes," do you believe
this statement? You may say, "Yes Lord, all things are possible with
you, but not with me." Or you may say, "I do believe your words,
but you are not here." Like the boy's father, you would say, "I do
believe, but please help my unbelief." Do you see the self-contra-
diction in his statement? While he did believe, he did not actually
believe.

The father of the boy must have lived a wretched life because
his son was not normal. Whenever the unclean spirit seized and
threw his son into a convulsion, the father might have felt that

he would rather die than live and have to see the pain of his son. When he heard that Jesus could heal any sickness, even demon possession, he went out to meet Jesus in hopes of healing his son. When he arrived, Jesus was not there. He became even more disheartened when the disciples failed to heal his son. Perhaps his unbelief rooted from this. If such was the case, what did he believe—that Jesus could heal any sickness, the word of God, or that all things are possible to believers? What does it mean to believe?

If you go to any of the mainstream churches, you will hear a very familiar message: "when you accept Christ in faith as your Savior, you become a child of God. Now you are a new creature. When you come across difficult times, just trust in God." This kind of message gives us more of a dilemma rather than comfort and answers. Why doesn't the Almighty God protect His children? Why does God allow terrible things to happen to His beloved sons and daughters? The Bible says that all things possible are to those who believe, yet why do we not see anything happen? People say that part of life is facing trials. We all live accepting these conditions. Even among believers, there is hardly anyone that lives with the constant joy and thankfulness the Bible says we should. Instead, many believers live in a constant state of worry and concern. Most have come to accept worry as a normal state of life. We know that babies feel secure and at peace in their mothers' arms. By the same token, children of God, who have the genuine faith, should never live in anxiety about tomorrow.

That is why Jesus accentuates that we cannot enter the kingdom of Heaven unless we become like children (Matt 18:3). If you are anxious for any reason, you do not have proper faith (Eph 2:8). Romans 15:13 tells us that all joy and peace comes only when we truly believe: "Now may the God of hope fill you with all joy and peace in believing, that you may abound in hope by the power of the Holy Spirit." This means that if you had the right faith, you would truly be joyful and at peace. In other words, if you do not have happiness and peace, that is an indicator that you do not have the proper faith. You have already fallen from faith. I am sure there are those who will be startled at such a statement. How can it be that if you dutifully attend church and consider yourself to have faith that this statement could apply to you?

Once again, there isn't a definite answer. Perhaps you are under the assumption that you have already become a child of God. What if it is not as you think? You might say that you've already accepted Jesus as your Savior and go to church every Sunday. Even if you are not a perfect person, you consider yourself not such a bad person. You might think that you are not like others: criminals, murderers, and adulterers. What kind of faith do you have? According to 2 Corinthians 13:5, faith is Jesus Christ in you, not simply believing. To make sure you have faith, you should test yourself: "Test yourselves to see if you are in the faith; examine yourselves! Or do you not recognize this about yourselves, that Jesus Christ is in you—unless indeed you fail the test?"

If we only have to believe once to be saved forever, then why is God stating that we could fail the test of whether we are in the faith or not? The audience to whom this word is applicable is not only non-believers, but also the believers, as this was written to the Christians at Corinth.

Instead of following the Bible's teaching, many churches automatically consider members believers. This verse states that "You believe that God is one. You do well; the demons also believe, and shudder" (Jas 2:19). What the Scripture says here is that even demons believe. Unlike demons, there is no fear in church goers' love. However, believing or confessing with your own knowledge is not faith. That is why so many of those we call Christians end up in corruption and all kinds of sins. Faith is the gift of God, not what we believe. God gives faith to anyone who follows the way of the Bible. Ephesians 2:8 states, "For by grace you have been saved through faith; and not of yourselves, it is the gift of God."

Let's be unbiased and search for the truth in the Bible. 1 Timothy 6:10 states that the love of money will cause you to wander you away from the faith and pierce you with many worries and anxieties. Thus, having worries and anxieties is evidence that you do not have proper faith. Furthermore, 1 Timothy 4:1–2 states that those who fall away from the faith will end up paying attention to deceitful spirits and living a hypocritical life. In truth, it is not only the scribes and the Pharisees that are hypocritical, but also those who attend church who are not true Christians. These people do not actually have faith even if they think or claim they do. They profess to be good Christians and yet do not forgive others in their heart. They commit sins with their hearts and minds, but outwardly they pretend to be clean. Are you one of these people? Aside from that verse, there are numerous other Bible verses that claim we could lose our faith. For example, Ezekiel 33:13–20 clearly shows us that when the righteous commit sin, they shall surely die in it, unless there is repentance.

It is very clear that God will judge you based on your current behavior, regardless of what has been committed or forgiven in the past. Even though the way of God is very clear in Scripture, it is sad to see many church goers insist on their teachings and the interpretation of their denominations. Do not be deceived. Just because you attend church does not mean you have faith. Faith is not something you can acquire or relinquish on your own. Even when we claim that we have faith and that we believe in Him, many still experiences lives filled with problems and worries. There is definitely something wrong with this picture. People say that the reason for this is our lack of faith. While this is true, the real reason is that there has been no faith to begin with or it has already been lost through unrepented sin. Many are familiar with the above verses and have tried very hard to live according to those verses by completely relying on God. However, they are unsuccessful, resorting to excuses and dismissing the Old Testament.

Whoever chooses to believe that all of God's messages, principles and truths are somehow debased because they do not come from their "preferred" Testament, believes that the Bible is a historical book and not the book of promise from the God Almighty. The joyful and peaceful life is life in faith. Ask yourself: do you have worries and anxieties? Do you have complaints and strife? In your heart, do you worry about your children? Are there times when you are not at peace and are upset? These are all indicators that you are not in faith. Ask yourself honestly if you are living according to the Bible. You have to discern the difference between living a life in the faith versus one that is not. This can mean the difference between going to Heaven or Hell.

There are many stories of Pharisees and scribes in the four Gospels of the New Testament. Pharisees and scribes were well-educated experts of the Law and leaders in society. They were committed believers of God willing to travel around on sea and land to make one proselyte (Matt 23:15). They were also proud descendants of Abraham. Outwardly, they were very sincere religious people fasting twice a week and paying tithes of their earnings. They despised swindlers, the unjust, adulterers, and tax collectors who worked for the Roman government. Pharisees and the scribes were ethically and morally superior to other groups of people. However, in Matthew 5:20, Jesus says that our righteousness should be better than that of Pharisees and the scribes to enter the kingdom of Heaven: "For I say to you that unless your righteousness surpasses that of the scribes and Pharisees, you will not enter the kingdom of heaven."

How can our righteousness be better than that of the scribes and Pharisees? Once again, I ask you not to rely on your own thoughts or others' teaching, only Scripture. Jesus clearly shows how our righteousness could surpass that of the scribes and Pharisees. It is a teaching of Jesus that when you repent and become humble, you are justified and your righteousness is better than that of the scribes and Pharisees (Luke 18:14). Unfortunately, some churches will teach that you are already righteous and saved. If this is true, why does Jesus tell us that we will not enter the kingdom of Heaven unless our righteousness surpasses that of the scribes and Pharisees? Some may quote Romans 10:10 to vehemently deny the need for repentance to enter Heaven. According to this verse, when you believe with your heart, you will be righteous, and when you confess with your mouth, you will be saved. But can you differ between believing with your heart and remembering with your brain? According to the book of Jeremiah, your heart is 'more deceitful than all else' (Jer 17:9). People's hearts are unsteady, unreliable, and easily broken. Faith means that Jesus Christ is in you

(2 Cor 13:5). Jesus Christ will not stay in an unclean and deceitful heart. Faith is the gift of God (Eph 2:8), not what you claim.

This is the word of God, but in conjunction with the rest of the Scripture. Cherry picking verses is dangerous. Why does God provide us with 66 Testaments? If you stick to one or two verses and ignore the rest, this is a serious offense according to Revelation:

> I testify to everyone who hears the words of the prophecy of this book: if anyone adds to them, God will add to him the plagues which are written in this book; and if anyone takes away from the words of the book of this prophecy, God will take away his part from the tree of life and from the holy city, which are written in this book. (Rev 22:18–19)

The young boy in Mark 9 was completely healed. The boy's father was extremely fortunate to meet Jesus and receive His prayer. Where or how do you meet Jesus? After His resurrection, Jesus "sat down at the right hand of God" according to Mark 16:19. In the near future, we are going to see Him just as He is under one condition: that we are purified. In order to see Him, we should not have sins (1 John 3:6). That is why we need the blood of Christ (Eph 1:7). That is why Jesus was born the Messiah/Christ (Matt 1:16) and died as Christ (Rom 5:8). What we need at this moment is Christ's blood. Sadly, people do not realize how they should see Jesus in their life. Without knowing anything, people just call Jesus' name. That is why even if they call to Jesus all day long, they do not receive answers to their prayers. After the young boy was healed, the disciples privately asked Jesus, "Why could we not drive it out?" Jesus answered them, "This kind cannot come out by anything but prayer" (Mark 9:29). In Matthew, Jesus explained that His disciples did not have enough faith to heal the young boy. Thus, when you have little faith, your prayer will not be answered. In order to have more faith, you need repentance in prayer. Romans 10:17 says, "So faith comes from hearing, and hearing by the word of Christ." It is not just the word, but the word of Christ. God gives His word to people as the Law to expose our sins. After repenting your sins with the Law, the Law will become the word of

Christ. Your prayers will be answered when you continue to pray by repenting your sins and meditating on the Law.

CHAPTER 3

NEW COVENANT

· ·

THE INIQUITIES OF OUR FATHERS

K OREA has a very gloomy history during the early 20th cen-
tury. In 1910, Korea lost their territory to Japan. There was
no more Korean government, and even the country was no longer called Korea. The Japanese prohibited the Korean language,
forcing everyone to learn Japanese. Young men were coerced to
fight in the Japanese army. Young women were taken from their
homes to become "comfort women" for the Japanese army, or sex
slaves. Refusal of the Japanese's demands resulted in torture and
death. My father's generation intensely hated the Japanese because
of all that has happened. They said they would never forgive the
Japanese. Even now, many Koreans do not forgive the Japanese
for their acts. When I learned of this history at school, I also was
enraged. I wondered why such horrible things happened to my
country. I do not intend to share the entire history of Korea, but
I believe that history tells us valuable lessons; what our ancestors
saw and what we now reap (Gal 6:7).

Before Korea was annexed to Japan, God sent many missionaries to Korea. More than twenty thousand accepted God's love
through the missionaries' sacrificial efforts. However, Korea's xe-
nophobic ruler, King Lee of the Lee dynasty, persecuted believers

and killed missionaries. Korean leaders not only betrayed God, but also killed many innocent people. Within fifty years, the Korean people received what their ancestors had sown.

In the Old Testament, God used His prophets to warn the Israeli people. Whenever the Israeli disobeyed the word of God or betrayed His love, the Lord used stronger countries to attack them and rule over them as reproof and discipline. When they repined from their misfortunes, it was too late. God's anger was all upon Israel. Their families became slaves. The women were ravished by the enemies. Many of them were killed by the unmerciful hand of foreign rulers. The prophet Jeremiah prayed:

> Our fathers sinned, and are no more; It is we who have borne their iniquities. Slaves rule over us; There is no one to deliver us from their hand. We get our bread at the risk of our lives Because of the sword in the wilderness. Our skin has become as hot as an oven, Because of the burning heat of famine. (Lam 5:7–10)

Have you lamented your life because so many misfortunes have befallen you? Have you complained to your parents, to God, or to someone else because your life looked unfair in comparison to another's? Have your illnesses, misfortunes, divorces, or unemployment dismayed you? Have you thought about why some children are born into rich families, others into poor families, and why some are successful, while others are failures? We usually consider it luck, but indeed it is not a matter of fate or luck, but one of our forefathers' iniquities. The Bible clearly shows us that iniquities, our forefathers' sins, came upon us and made our life miserable: "But as for you, your corpses will fall in this wilderness. 'Your sons shall be shepherds for forty years in the wilderness, and they will suffer for your unfaithfulness, until your corpses lie in the wilderness" (Num 14:32–33).

Then again, most churches ignore these verses as well because they belong to the Old Testament. Do you believe that the Almighty God is the only God, and that He has not changed? If so, His words should remain the same yesterday, today, and forever. That is why the prophet Isaiah asked the people of God to declare their fathers' sins (Isa 58:1), and the prophet Jeremiah prayed and lamented their forefathers' iniquities. Only God can control a human being's life.

Today, doctors ask you about your parents' medical history. Because your DNA constitution, structure, and genes come from your parents, your parents' medical history is very important in predicting the inclinations of your body. If your parents have allergies, you have a very high chance of having the same symptoms. Interestingly enough, the Bible revealed this idea a long time ago:

> If you address as Father the One who impartially judges according to each one's work, conduct yourselves in fear during the time of your stay on earth; knowing that you were not redeemed with perishable things like silver or gold from your futile way of life inherited from your forefathers, but with precious blood, as of a lamb unblemished and spotless, the blood of Christ. (1 Pet 1: 17–19)

According to this verse, much of your way of life has been handed down to you from your ancestors. In other words, whatever your forefathers sowed is inherited by their offspring to the third and the fourth generations:

> You shall not worship them or serve them; for I, the Lord your God, am a jealous God, visiting the iniquity of the fathers on the children, on the third and the fourth generations of those who hate Me, but showing lovingkindness to thousands, to those who love Me and keep My commandments. (Exod 20:5–6)

Parents love their children and expect successful futures. However, if parents knew the word of God, they would not commit any sins against the Lord. They would repent their sins for their children. Instead, they unknowingly send their iniquities to their children and grandchildren. Instead of lovingkindness for thousands, people choose punishment to the third and fourth generations, due to ignorance of the word of God. What a pitiful situation! Exodus also confirms that the iniquity of fathers will be on the children and on the grandchildren to the third and fourth generations:

> Then the Lord passed by in front of him and proclaimed, "The Lord, the Lord God, compassionate and gracious, slow to anger, and abounding in lovingkindness and truth; who keeps lovingkindness for thousands, who forgives iniquity, transgression and sin; yet He will by no means leave the guilty unpunished, visiting the iniquity of fathers on the children and on the grandchildren to the third and fourth generations. (Exod 34:6–7)

We come into this world with the sins of our fathers. Even before we are actually born, we already have an immeasurable amount of sin. Most people think that babies are innocent. Yet this is not true, because of the sins from their ancestors. Recall King David's sin. Not only did he sleep with Uriah's wife, Bathsheba, he also killed Uriah by sending him into battle after finding out about Bathsheba's pregnancy. However, the newborn baby died because of David's sin.

As already noted, this is the teaching of the Bible, the word of God. It's the reason why some babies have congenital disease or deformities. In other words, we could help prevent abnormalities if we follow the path of repentance and the promise of God. The problem is that most people, including Christians, do not believe the word of God Almighty, "For You formed my inward parts; You wove me in my mother's womb" (Ps 139:13), and "Yet You are He who brought me forth from the womb; You made me trust when upon my mother's breasts" (Ps 22:9). It is the Lord who formed us in our mothers' wombs. It is the same Lord who brought us safely from the womb. Your mother or doctor cannot control your life, intelligence, constitution or character.

There was a boy named Peter. When he was born, he looked like a normal baby, but when he was four years old, his mother found out he was extremely intelligent. Despite this, his behavior was not normal; he suffered from attention deficiency, and was sometimes violent and hyper. His parents were very disappointed. He had to change schools many times due to his abnormal manner. Ordinarily, he was a very polite and shy kid, but whenever he was irritated, his temper got the better of him and he became a different person. His parents heard the mystery of Christ. They learned that they not only needed to repent their sins, but also the sins of their ancestors. As they began to seriously repent, within two years, God healed Peter. He did not need to attend different schools anymore and his entire personality changed. Everybody that knew him was surprised but very happy for him. It is one of the best examples of such a change that I have ever witnessed. As we know, special education cannot heal disabled children. Teachers take good care of their students, but cannot change their lives. Only God can change lives through the mystery of Christ. Do you have any idea how your ancestors lived? Probably not. The bottom line is that our ancestors handed down so many sins that control our lives. However, we can now receive blessings without following tradition. The word of God is more important than our traditions.

A few years ago, I had the chance to travel to several European countries. Back then, whenever I had time, I used to visit as many churches as possible. Every church I visited had spectacular architectural design, beautiful interiors, very expensive statues, and huge open spaces. Yet most churches were almost empty, even on Sunday. There were many sight-seeing travelers like me, but very few church members who attended regularly, according to the church pastors I spoke with. What's more is that most of those who did attend were elderly. It is apparent that when those churches were built, there were many church members who were able to support such vast, expensive buildings. Where are they now? Why could they not hand their faith to their posterity? My personal belief is that those church pastors did not teach about repentance of sins that sully the human soul and attract all sorts of iniquities and catastrophes if they are not repented. Therefore, those church members did not learn why bad things happen to "good" people. This was responsible for the decline of so many churches and denominations. Many reports and surveys have found that mainline Protestant churches in America are also losing their church members rapidly.

Jesus quoted Isaiah to rebuke the Pharisees' hypocrisy: "You hypocrites, rightly did Isaiah prophesy of you: 'THIS PEOPLE HONORS ME WITH THEIR LIPS, BUT THEIR HEART IS FAR AWAY FROM ME. 'BUT IN VAIN DO THEY WORSHIP ME, TEACHING AS DOCTRINES THE PRECEPTS OF MEN'" (Matt 15:7–9). Teaching dogmas in the name of tradition at the church is not uncommon. Without sermons based on the teachings of Christ, the Church will neither be blessed nor be called the body of Christ. Sermons should depend on changing human traditions that will make people aware of worldly sins that will eventually ruin church members' faith.

ACHIEVING COMPLETE VICTORY

There is a famous man in the Old Testament named David. One day his father asked him to visit his brothers who were in a battle against the Philistines. When David arrived at the battlefield, he saw the Philistine's champion, a giant named Goliath who challenged the army of Saul, king of Israel at the time. The Israelites knew that Goliath was stronger than they were. Even though Goliath insulted God and the Israelite army, no one wanted to fight with him. David volunteered to fight Goliath. Many people laughed at him, including his own brothers. David persuaded Saul to let him fight by telling him that when he kept sheep, he fought bears and lions using stones. He said,

> The Lord who delivered me from the paw of the lion and from the paw of the bear, He will deliver me from the hand of this Philistine. (1 Sam 17:37)

Saul allowed him to fight Goliath, lending him a garment, bronze helmet and armor. But David told Saul, "I cannot go with this for I have not tested them." David took them off. Then he took his stick in his hand, chose five smooth stones from the brook and put them in his shepherd's bag. He approached the Philistine. When Goliath saw David, he laughed at him,

Am I a dog, that you come to me with sticks?" And the Philistine cursed David by his gods. The Philistine also said to David, "Come to me, and I will give your flesh to the birds of the sky and the beasts of the field." Then David said to the Philistine, "You come to me with a sword, a spear, and a javelin, but I come to you in the name of the Lord of hosts, the God of the armies of Israel, whom you have taunted. (1 Sam 17: 43–45)

David put a stone in his sling and threw the stone at Goliath. The stone hit Goliath in the forehead and he fell instantly. When the Philistines saw that Goliath was dead, they ran for their lives. The Israelites gained a complete victory. Many preachers refer to David's story as an example of how Christians can achieve victory in their daily lives by trusting the Lord. Although the Israelite army believed in the Almighty God, they were very afraid when they saw Goliath. Fear was a critical component in a fight against Goliath. How David prevail? Not only did he trust God, he also was not afraid of Goliath. In other words, boldness is the key to gaining a complete triumph against all life matters. Proverbs states:

The wicked flee when no one is pursuing, But the righteous are bold as a lion. (Prov 28:1)

Thus, when you have sins, you will lose boldness. No one is righteous, not even a single person (Rom 3:10). Righteousness is a gift from God through Christ, the mystery of Christ. No one except David fully trusted the Lord. 1 John states,

There is no fear in love; but perfect love casts out fear, because fear involves punishment, and the one who fears is not perfected in love. (1 John 4:18)

If people declare that they believe in and love God, yet live in fear, this is a contradiction. In the Old Testament, the Israelites lost the promise of God even after He promised the land of Canaan. By the Lord's commandment, Moses sent the leaders of the Israelite tribes to scope out the Promised Land (Num 13:1–30). When they returned, there were two different reports. Only Caleb and Joshua gave a positive response. The rest delivered a negative report, comparing themselves to grasshoppers:

> So they gave out to the sons of Israel a bad report of the land which they had spied out, saying, "The land through which we have gone, in spying it out, is a land that devours its inhabitants; and all the people whom we saw in it are men of great size. "There also we saw the Nephilim (the sons of Anak are part of the Nephilim); and we became like grasshoppers in our own sight, and so we were in their sight. (Num 13: 32–33)

The Israelites raised their voices and wept all night long. Instead of trusting the promise of the Lord, they became afraid. As a result, they were barred from entering the Promised Land. It is tragic that they rebelled against God, wanting to return to Egypt to live as slaves. Even after they witnessed so many signs and wonders from the Lord, they still did not believe in Him. They continued to complain in the wilderness about the lack of water and food. God led them through the wilderness with a cloud by day and a column of fire at night, protecting them. However, the Israelites fell into sin, grumbling and complaining. They rejected the Promised Land, fearing people rather than God. How can you keep boldness in your daily life? The short answer is repentance.

The second major factor in retaining your boldness is to trust the word of God, just as Joshua and Caleb did. To know the word of God is not the same as trusting in the promise of God. Many Christians read the Bible every day and participate in Bible study. However, few people witness the promise of God coming true in their daily lives. The Pharisees knew the Scripture very well. However, they did not see that Jesus is the son of God and Christ. When the magi from the east came to Jerusalem to worship the newborn king of the Jews, King Herod asked all the chief priests and scribes where the Messiah was to be born. Since the chief priests and scribes knew the Scripture very well, they told King Herod (Matt 2:4–6). They did not know Christ was born and did not see the sign of the Messiah's birth like the magi foreigners did. All Scripture is inspired by God (2 Tim 3:16). You should not try to understand the word of God with your wisdom. Saul (later Apostle Paul), as an expert of the Law and zeal, harshly persecuted Christians. After repentance, the Apostle Paul testified that his eyes were opened and he started to see the will of the Lord by revelation. The will of God is hidden from the wise and intelligent (Matt 11:25). The word of God will not be known to your wisdom and knowledge (1 Cor 1:21). Memorizing goes to your head, not your heart. The Pharisees knew everything in the Bible, but they killed the Messiah in spiritual blindness.

The Apostle Peter confessed that Jesus was the Christ, and Jesus told him that he was blessed. However, he denied Jesus three times. All of Jesus' disciples ran away in fear. In the same way, all of us can still be caught by the world again. That is why we must repent the sins from our hearts every day. Psalm 119 tells us how we can escape from sin:

> Your word I have treasured in my heart, That I may not
> sin against You. (Ps 119:11)

If you do not treasure His word in your hearts, you become like the Pharisees who thought they were righteous and committed hypocritical acts. They knew all the rules and laws but committed sin and killed their Messiah. God set up a new covenant with Israel so they could keep the Law, instead of memorizing the Law. Only with the new covenant will the word enter your heart.

> Behold, days are coming," declares the Lord, "when I will make a new covenant with the house of Israel and with the house of Judah, not like the covenant which I made with their fathers in the day I took them by the hand to bring them out of the land of Egypt, My covenant which they broke, although I was a husband to them," declares the Lord. "But this is the covenant which I will make with the house of Israel after those days," declares the Lord, "I will put My law within them and on their heart I will write it; and I will be their God, and they shall be My people. (Jer 31:31–33)

The new covenant was completed when Jesus died for us and gave His body and blood. Eucharist performed by churches is a symbol of the new covenant. However, the real meaning of the bread and cup is that you are in Christ and Christ in you.

> So Jesus said to them, "Truly, truly, I say to you, unless you eat the flesh of the Son of Man and drink His blood, you have no life in yourselves. He who eats My flesh and drinks My blood has eternal life, and I will raise him up on the last day. For My flesh is true food, and My blood is true drink. He who eats My flesh and drinks My blood abides in Me, and I in him. (John 6: 53–56)

If you stay outside the Lord, you cannot bear the kind of fruit God is looking for. You must abide in Christ first. Then the Lord will be in you. If you are not abiding in Christ, you will be thrown away and dried up (John 15:6). If your life is dried up and full of anxiety, you are definitely outside of Christ, even if you go to church and read the Bible every day. How do you abide in Christ? It is only by the mystery of Christ, which is to be cleansed with the blood of Christ in repentance. When you are in Christ, Christ will be in you, which is the glory of the mystery God revealed to us (Col 1:27). Deuteronomy states:

> But the word is very near you, in your mouth and in your heart, that you may observe it (Deut 30:14)

The word is God (John 1:1). You can come near God in Christ by the blood of Christ (Eph 2:13). Then, the word will be in you so that you can observe it. The Scripture consistently reveals how Christians keep the command of God and receive the glory of hope. However, churches have ignored this message. So many church goers suffer without the glory of hope, which is not much different from non-believers. When you are outside of Christ, the covenants of promise do not belong to you. You do not have any hope and live without God in the world, even if you claim to believe in God (Eph 2:12). It is tragic to see people living without the help of the Lord perform hypocritical acts. When you live outside Christ, you may easily fall into earthly desire, which is an adulterer's sin against God (Jas 4:4). Colossians displays sins which bring God's wrath:

> Therefore consider the members of your earthly body as dead to immorality, impurity, passion, evil desire, and greed, which amounts to idolatry. For it is because of these things that the wrath of God will come upon the sons of disobedience, (Col 3:5–6)

God's wrath will come upon those who disobey, because of the sins of immorality that amount to idolatry. If you have greed, it is tantamount to idolatry. If you do not repent these sins, God's wrath will come upon you just as the Scripture indicates. However, if you keep repenting, you will be in Christ and Christ will enter your heart. You are able to worship God without receiving any wrath.

The Law was given through Moses (John 1:17). Why was the Law given? Romans 3:20 says that the Law was given to us in order for us to realize our sins. However, the Pharisees tried to keep the Law instead of realizing their sins. Jesus condemned the scribes and the Pharisees seated themselves in the chair of Moses (Matt 23:2). The scribes and the Pharisees asked people to keep the Law. However, the scribes and the Pharisees were not able to observe the Law themselves. Matthew points out:

> therefore all that they tell you, do and observe, but do not do according to their deeds; for they say things and do not do them. They tie up heavy burdens and lay them on men's shoulders, but they themselves are unwilling to move them with so much as a finger. (Matt 23:3–4)

Church leaders instruct to love one's neighbor. But even they cannot love their congregations, leading to denominations. Why? Like the scribes and Pharisees, they know the word of God in their head. However, they do not know how to obey the command of God. Hosea clearly says that if you reject the Law of God, then He will reject you:

> My people are destroyed for lack of knowledge. Because you have rejected knowledge, I also will reject you from

being My priest. Since you have forgotten the law of your
God, I also will forget your children. (Hos 4:6)

If you pursue His righteousness and keep the truth in your
heart, complete victory will follow you.

ANXIETY-FREE LIFE

Do you believe you are going to do well because of your faith? In
reality, we often do not actually believe God. God can raise up the
dead and give to those who are lacking, but believers hold a lot of
doubt. Many believers think that God does not perform miracles
nowadays, leading to unbelief. Because their prayers do not seem
to be answered, people instead look toward other people for the
answer. Matthew provides a good tip on how people can live in
blessing:

> But blessed are your eyes, because they see; and your
> ears, because they hear. (Matt 13:16)

We should live the lives of the blessed if our eyes should see
and our ears should hear. You would say 'I am not blind,' as the
Pharisees protested. Jesus replied that because they claimed to see,
their sins remain (John 9:41). People who are able to see do not
know what is going to happen tomorrow. They can hear but they
do not understand the word. Matthew states,

> FOR THE HEART OF THIS PEOPLE HAS BECOME
> DULL, WITH THEIR EARS THEY SCARCELY HEAR,
> AND THEY HAVE CLOSED THEIR EYES, OTHER-
> WISE THEY WOULD SEE WITH THEIR EYES, HEAR
> WITH THEIR EARS, AND UNDERSTAND WITH
> THEIR HEART AND RETURN, AND I WOULD HEAL
> THEM. (Matt 13:15)

Because your heart has become dull, you cannot see or hear.
If you hate others, your eyes become dull (1 John 2:11). People are
unable to see because they do not repent their sins. When they are
in the darkness, their eyes worsen. The sins in your heart are the

cause of hatred. Psalm 6:7 states, "My eye has wasted away with grief; It has become old because of all my adversaries." Psalm 88:9 states, "My eye has wasted away because of affliction; I have called upon You every day, O Lord; I have spread out my hands to You." According to these Scriptures, there are many reasons why you cannot see. The only way to reopen your eyes is to remove the dullness in your heart. If you keep dullness in your heart, your life will be filled with unhappiness. When people are faced with difficulties, they start to complain or worry. People tend to only be grateful when good things happen. However, when the Scripture says, "be anxious for nothing," (Phil 4;6–7) there should be a way to overcome all anxieties and to live successful lives as the Lord promises. To see whether you are following God or not, ask yourself if you are at peace. If your hearts are not at peace, you lose to demons. The way to defeat Satan is to be alert, and the way to be alert is through thanksgiving. Colossians 4:2 states, "Devote yourselves to prayer, keeping alert in it with an attitude of thanksgiving;"

When we do not give thanks, we become prey for Satan. Even when we fall, we can repent and become thankful again. The way to win over demons is by the word of God.

In order to humble yourself, you must repent. If you remain thankful, you will always prosper. If you are not alert, you will be attacked by snakes. We do not live by bread alone but by the word of God. We must become people who can consume the word as spiritual food. That is why prayer, supplication, and thanksgiving are essential for attaining the peace of God. With prayer and supplication with thanksgiving, God will not only give us what we pray for, but also watch over our hearts and minds. That is important because life comes from our hearts. Our minds are constantly distracted and worried, and we cannot watch over our hearts ourselves. That is why prayer and thanksgiving is so precious, because only the Lord can help us.

Deuteronomy provides another tip on how we can overcome anxiety and avoid the mistakes of the Israelites:

> You shall remember all the way which the Lord your
> God has led you in the wilderness these forty years, that

> He might humble you, testing you, to know what was in your heart, whether you would keep His commandment or not. And He humbled you and let you be hungry, and fed you with manna which you did not know, nor did your fathers know, that not live by bread alone, but man lives by everything that proceeds out of mouth of the Lord. (Deut 8:2–3)

The Israelites were separated into two groups: those who held onto God, and those who were destroyed. This verse says to "remember the way which the Lord your God has led you in the wilderness." God wants us to remember this. Why did He lead His people through the wilderness? He did it to humble them, and to know whether they would keep His commandments. In addition to these, God wants to teach us to live by everything that comes out of the mouth of the Lord.

Complaining and worrying about your life is a form of arrogance, because you're trying to live your own life. When something doesn't work out, we tend to look at the past and complain about our current situation. Instead, we must humble ourselves and keep His commandments. That is, we need to live like true people and obey His word. Even though the Lord miraculously led the people of Israel and protected them in the wilderness, the Israelites were unable to humble themselves, and instead they grumbled and tested God, looking back toward Egypt and the past. Instead of moving forward to a better place, they were tied to their old lives, so they were stuck in the wilderness. They did not believe the promise of God and despised the love of God in the wilderness. As a result of peevishness, thousands of Israelites were bitten to death by snakes.

When thanksgiving disappears, anxiety will start to control your life. Forty years is not a short time. If you live in grumbling and anxiety, you will waste your life. How can we live a grateful life, in other words, a humble life in front of God? The answer is we should not live by bread alone, but by everything that proceeds out of the mouth of the Lord. Those who live by bread alone are like beasts. To live like true human beings is to live by every word that proceeds out of the mouth of the Lord. You might say 'I read the Bible every day.' Reading the Bible, however, is not same as meditating on the Law. The Bible is not a novel, but spiritual food. When you meditate on the Law, the Law will be living spiritual food and provide wisdom and understanding. Psalm 119:147–148 says: "I rise before dawn and cry for help: I wait for Thy words. My eyes anticipate the night watches, that I may mediate Thy word." When you meditate on the word of God, your dullness will disappear. You will be able to see the promise of God in your life and hear the loving voice of the Lord. Your life will be blessed without any difficulties and anxieties. You can recover what you lost. Romans 15:13 states, "Now may the God of hope fill you with all joy and peace in believing, so that you will abound in hope by the power of the Holy Spirit."

Those in the faith have joy and peace. If we are not joyful or peaceful, we are away from the faith. You may have had a tranquil heart yesterday, but that does not guarantee you will be peaceful today. 2 Corinthians 13:5 says to "test yourself to see if you are in the faith; examine yourself!" If you were not able to lose your faith, the Bible would not say this. King Saul and Solomon in the Bible believed, but they fell away. Even if you have many successes and a comfortable life, you can still fail to have peace. If you keep repenting with tears and giving thanks, the first thing you will receive is a joyful and peaceful mind. Then, great things from God will follow.

God's will for you is to give thanks in everything (1 Thess 5:16–18). If any little thing bothers you, you lose your thanksgiving, so how is this possible? You must repent your sins. This is the sign of Jonah. When the Pharisees asked Jesus for a sign, He said the only sign was the sign of Jonah (Matt 12:38–39). Jonah was in the belly of the fish for three days, but with thanksgiving he was able to live. When you are metaphorically in the belly of the fish, whatever your situation, even if it's only for 10 minutes you might complain about it. With repentance, Jonah was able to give thanks and God helped him get out of the fish. If bad events occur and your heart is no longer at peace, you need to realize that you've departed from the faith and repent again. According to Deuteronomy, there are two paths:

> See, I have set before you today life and prosperity, and death and adversity (Deut 30:15)

Unfortunately, the Israelites chose death and adversity. Nowadays, many believers unintentionally go to the way of death and adversity, either by flawed church dogma or depraved preaching. Verse 16 states:

> in that I command you today to love the Lord your God, to walk in His ways and to keep His commandments and His statutes and His judgments, that you may live and multiply, and that the Lord your God may bless you in the land where you are entering to possess it. (Deut 30:16)

How do we go the way of life and prosperity? The first thing is to love God. What does it mean to love God? Does it mean going to church more often? Does it mean praying to God frequently? The Bible clearly states that to love God means to receive forgiveness for your sins. Those who receive more forgiveness love God more. Luke 7:47 states, "For this reason I say to you, her sins, which are many, have been forgiven, for she loved much: but he who is forgiven little, loves little." Furthermore, to love God is to keep His commandments (John 14:21), which are to love God with all your heart, soul, mind, and strength, and to love your neighbor (Mark 12:30–31). Our sinful nature leads us to have friendship with the world instead of God (Jas 4:4). That is why repentance is the way to love God and to live a life in prosperity. We cannot see what will happen tomorrow. Natural disasters, accidents, and death occur—but death and life are in the hand of God. What we need to do is leave the love of the world and hold onto God. Even Abram doubted. He wasn't faithful from the beginning. If you falter, you can repent again. If you do not obey the word, you will have difficulties. Let us obey the word and repent our sins so that we can love God, and God will protect us. Give thanks and glorify God, and the Lord will lead you to life and prosperity.

THE FEAR OF THE LORD

When the earth was corrupt in the sight of God, God was looking for a righteous man to build an ark. His name was Noah. Noah was godly and blameless in his time. God told him to build an ark, and showed Noah exactly how to build it. Although everyone thought Noah was out of his mind, he obeyed God and did as told. Noah prepared the ark in the fear of the Lord for the salvation of his household (Heb 11:7).

Many lose their lives through accidents, disease, or natural disasters. Why does God allow this? What God commanded the Israelites was to learn the fear of the Lord and teach their children to fear God. As the word of God promises, when you fear God, you will not be touched by evil. Proverbs 19:23 states, "The fear of the Lord leads to life, so that one may sleep satisfied, untouched by evil." We need the fear of the Lord. Proverbs 8:13 states, "The fear of the Lord is to hate evil; Pride and arrogance and the evil way, and the perverted mouth, I hate."

What does it mean to hate evil? This refers to cleansing your sins with the blood of Christ. People do not realize that the love of money is the root of all sorts of evil (1 Tim 6:10). People live for money, even hating, fighting, and killing because of money. Whenever you have friendship with the world, you are hostile toward God (Jas 4:4). God promises that when you seek His kingdom, then everything—whatever you eat, drink, and wear—will be added unto you (Matt 6:33). All these things are necessary for life. But if you do not have the first, most important thing, then it is all for nothing. First, you must seek His kingdom and His righteousness. If you don't know this verse well, you won't know how to live. It doesn't matter if you speak it or sing it if you can't live it. What is His kingdom? Romans 14:17 states, "For the kingdom of God is not eating and drinking, but righteousness and peace and joy in the Holy Spirit. For he who in this way serves Christ is acceptable to God and approved by men."

If you do not seek His kingdom daily, you easily become a slave of money. Every day we struggle, lacking peace and joy while asleep or awake. Even babies wake up crying because they're looking for their mother. Because of the root of all sorts of evil in your heart, you are not at peace and don't have joy. Parents can feed their children, but children's growth comes from God. The sorrow and anxiety of the world leads to death. We have two options: to fear the Lord, or not. Fearing the Lord leads to a satisfied life, filled with happiness, seeking His kingdom first and His righteousness. What does it mean to live righteously? How do we gain righteousness? Not through prayer or singing hymns. The answer is in the word: by seeking His kingdom through repentance. God's will is to pray without ceasing and give thanks.

God is patient. Every day we build up wrath and destruction and we reap what we sow. The only way to clean ourselves of these things is through the blood of Christ. No matter how many sins you have built up, with the blood of Christ they are washed away. Isaiah 1:18 states, "Come now, and let us reason together," Says the Lord, "Though your sins are as scarlet, They will be as white as snow; Though they are red like crimson, They will be like wool."

What is righteousness? Sheep are righteous (Matt 25:33–41). The sheep shall go to the right and the goats to the left to be judged. Living as the righteous means living like sheep do. Sheep are those led by the Shepherd. They don't live alone. If a sheep is left unprotected by a Shepherd, it is vulnerable to predators. So, if we receive protection and follow the Shepherd, we are like sheep. Psalm 34:9 states, "O fear the Lord, you His saints; For to those who fear Him there is no want." Those who fear Him shall have no want. Sheep are those who hate evil and fear the Lord, and they will be protected from any hardship. Sheep also know their shepherd so they're not afraid of him. Proverbs 28:14 states, "How blessed is the man who fears always, But he who hardens his heart will fall into calamity." If you do not fear the Lord always, your hearts become hardened and you fall into calamity. Without God's protection, you are prone to disaster. Now that you understand what it means to first seek His kingdom and His righteousness, it boils down to repentance and thanksgiving.

In the Old Testament, Abram (who eventually became Abraham) lived in Haran. God asked Abram to leave Haran when Abram was 75 years old. He left his home with the promise of God to make him a great nation. Abram's journey was sidetracked due to famine leading to Egypt. He went through many conflicts, even giving his wife to a Pharaoh to save his own life. God told Abraham that he would have a son, but Abraham did not believe, so he did not have a son for another 25 years. Since Abraham failed to wait for the promise of a child from the Lord, he had Ishmael, a child of the flesh by his maid Hagar, causing strife in his family. However, after Isaac was born, Abraham eventually obeyed God, offering Isaac as a burnt offering when commanded. God told him, "I know that you fear God" (Gen 22:12). Abraham took twenty-five years from believing in the Lord to fearing God.

In reality, we often do not actually believe God. When Abram was told that he would have a child at 99 years of age, he and his wife doubted. People who say they believe, don't really believe. God can raise up the dead and give to those who are lacking. Abraham made a very difficult decision to leave his homeland for the unknown. He actually believed in God's promise. How did Abraham not waver in unbelief to become the father of all believers? He feared God.

People will doubt and be disappointed with unwelcome circumstances. The key to overall victory is fearing God. The wicked are beset by harm, and God gives us these problems so that we can follow Him properly. If we repent and have the fear of the Lord, the blessings of Abram can be ours. Galatians 3:29 states, "And if you belong to Christ, then you are Abram's descendants, heirs according to promise." If you want to receive God's promise, you should belong to Christ, which is made possible through the mystery of Christ. Abraham's faith grew strong by fearing God. Romans testifies,

> Without becoming weak in faith he contemplated his own body, now as good as dead since he was about a hundred years old, and the deadness of Sarah's womb; yet, with respect to the promise of God, he did not waver

in unbelief but grew strong in faith, giving glory to God, and being fully assured that what God had promised, He was able also to perform. Therefore, it was also credited to him as righteousness. Now, not only for his sake was it written that it was credited to him, but for our sake also, to whom it will be credited, as those who believe in Him who raised Jesus our Lord from the dead. (Rom 4:19–24)

All we have to do is hold onto Him and not let go. Believing in God means that we have no need to believe in people. Solomon's father, David, committed many sins. However, David repented his sins thoroughly. As Matthew 1:1 attests, Abraham and David's names are recorded in the genealogy of Jesus the Messiah. In order to prevent wicked sins that weaken your faith, you must repent and fear God. With the fear of the Lord, you can overcome all things and become heirs of God's promise. When you repent, you become humble in front of the Lord. 1 Peter 5:6 states, "Therefore humble yourselves under the mighty hand of God, that He may exalt you at the proper time."

When God allows problems, He wants you to understand so that you may be exalted at the proper time. We should believe in God even when times are hard, having the same heart before Him regardless of how life is. People change all the time. We repent but when things don't seem to work out, we stop, or we forget when we begin to prosper and we become too busy. Our hearts become divided, and we begin betraying and disobeying. There are many promises in this Bible, and many churchg oers who read the Bible, but not everyone receives these promises. The Bible says that you will prosper, but people do not prosper and instead complain. The Bible says that you will be protected from evil, but people fall upon destruction easily. It says that the Lord is your shepherd, but people do not live like sheep.

The key is Christ, but people do not know whether they are in or outside of Christ. If you are outside of your house, it does not matter if the weather is nice, but when it rains or gets too hot or cold, you immediately realize that you are not indoors. If you look at the Bible, there are all sorts of positive messages about promises, but people do not take them seriously. If you have any doubt regarding God's promise, like Abram, you are outside of Christ. If you have anxiety, hate, or concerns, you are outside of Christ. In Christ, His promises are yes, and we say amen. That is how we glorify God.

> For as many as are the promises of God, in Him they are yes; therefore also through Him is our Amen to the glory of God through us. (2 Cor 1: 20)

People claim to live for the glory of God, but they do not know how. What does it mean to glorify God? To believe the word. If we believe the word then God will be pleased. Mary was a virgin when the angel Gabriel told her that she would have a baby. At the time, if a woman became pregnant out of wedlock she was killed. However, Mary believed in the promise of God and she gave birth to Jesus. 1 Thessalonians states,

> For this reason we also constantly thank God that when you received the word of God which you heard from us, you accepted it not as the word of men, but for what it really is, the word of God, which also performs its work in you who believe. (1 Thess 2:13)

If you believe, then His word will perform its work. All Scripture is inspired by God, not from people's minds (2 Tim 3:16). They are not the words of men, but the words of God. We must wait until the time is right. Even when people wait to receive blessings, they can still fall. When we are outside of Christ, how do we go in Christ? With thanksgiving after repentance, which is the mystery of Christ. If we always give thanks, we can be in Christ. With thanks, we enter the door of Christ. Test yourself to see if you are in Christ by seeing if you are thankful or have any complaints. Even if you are not, God will wait for you. Saying 'amen' means that you believe. Saying 'amen' to His word glorifies Him. Believing in His word pleases God. But outside of Christ, we are filled with doubt and cannot believe. In the New Testament, Peter was jailed. An angel came to him and told him to put on his shoes and walk out of the jail. When he was free, many people were not able to believe. 1 Corinthians states,

> Whether, then, you eat or drink or whatever you do, do all to the glory of God. Give no offense either to Jews or to Greeks or to the church of God; just as I also please all men in all things, not seeking my own profit but the profit of the many, so that they may be saved. (1 Cor 10:31–33)

No matter what you do, you should do it for the glory of God. If you look at verse 33, this is how you really glorify God. People who claim to glorify God often live for themselves. Truly glorifying God means to do things for other people's benefit, so that they can be saved. We must all prosper and receive the promises of God so that we can help others. 1 Timothy 2:4 states, "who desires all men to be saved and to come to the knowledge of the truth." If you do not know what God truly wants, you end up thinking that He only judges people. God is righteous and just. What God wants is for all men to be saved, and to come to the knowledge of the truth.

People can say 'amen' with their lips, but they do not believe in God or behave like believers. They believe in their own ideas and ways. If you prosper, you can help others and bring them back to God. That is what God wants. People who help one another in this way are people of light. Abraham struggled in his weak faith from Genesis chapter 12 to chapter 21. However, when he feared God in Genesis chapter 22, his eyes were opened and he was able to see the ram that the Lord prepared for him. So when you fear God, the Lord will open your eyes to see what God has prepared for you. "But just as it is written, "Things which eye has not seen and ear has not heard, and which have not entered the heart of man, all that God has prepared for those who love Him"" (1 Cor 2:9).

HEALTHY LIFE AND BEST MEDICINE

Even with our medical advancements, we can't stop disease. The key to be well in your body is a tranquil heart. Stress is extremely detrimental, and even if you are wealthy, your life will be miserable without your wellbeing. How do you maintain tranquility?

According to Proverbs 14:30, resentment rots the bones. If your bones rot, you cannot replenish your blood. Proverbs 17:22 also tells us that a broken spirit will dry up the bones, but a joyful heart is good medicine. The bone marrow loses its ability to produce new blood cells. Without this continual regeneration, you lose the ability to fight off diseases. Therefore, a joyful and cleansed heart is the key. This is not some theological conclusion, but rather the promise of God Almighty. When people are sick, they do not know that they can be healed by the word of God. Healing will happen if you trust the word of God. Proverbs reveals this:

> Do not be wise in your own eyes; Fear the Lord and turn away from evil. It will be healing to your body and refreshment to your bones. (Prov 3:7–8)

People tend to live by relying on their own wisdom. Even when the Almighty God offers guidance, many people ignore His promise and live however they like. After ruining their ways, people's hearts rage against the Lord (Prov 19:3). The Bible warns that if you try to succeed on your own, you will end up destroying your life (1 Tim 6:9). When people get older and are confronted with severe sickness, they begin to regret how they lived. It is not too late if you are determined to follow the promise of the Lord. Fearing the Lord and turning away from evil means repentance of your sins. When you repent, God will restore your faith and start to heal your sickness. In this healing process, the blood of Christ cures all sicknesses and chronic diseases. Those in the faith have joy and peace (Rom 15:13). One way to examine whether you are in the faith is to check the condition of your heart, whether you are peaceful or anxious. You may live a successful or comfortable life but still fail to have peace. If you keep repenting with tears and giving thanks, the first thing you receive is a joyful and peaceful mind. Great things from God follow.

Joseph was one of Jacob's twelve sons in the land of Canaan. Jacob loved Joseph more than his other sons. His brothers were jealous of Joseph. They all believed in God. Their grandparents, Abraham and Isaac were devoted men in front of God. Jacob met God and worshiped the Lord sincerely. Even so, Jacob's brothers could not avoid the sin of jealousy. When Jacob gave Joseph a new coat, this made his brothers even more jealous. They planned to get rid of him. How sinful to want to kill their own brother! Envy is a sin of hatred toward God coming from our reprobated mind (Rom 1:28–32). Instead of killing him as they had planned, they sold him to a caravan of Egyptian traders. In Egypt, Joseph became a slave to Potiphar, an Egyptian officer of Pharaoh, the captain of the bodyguard. However, Joseph didn't give up his life and didn't complain. Through ceaseless prayer, Joseph received grace from God. The Lord was with him, so he became a successful man. After interpreting the dreams of the Pharaoh, he became second-in-command. Joseph's story demonstrates how you can overcome obstacles and enemies present in your life. Romans 8:28 states, "And we know that God causes all things to work together for good to those who love God, to those who are called according to His purpose."

God causes all things to work together for good to those who love Him. Even if things don't seem to be working out right now, everything will turn out well. Even if you make enemies, if you pray, you can overcome them. You might be sick and anxious, but God makes everything work together for good. Joseph, who was sold into slavery, seemed to have a very troubled life. However, even though he was sold as a slave in Egypt, he was able to save Egypt and his people, working together for good just as God promised. In order to work together for good, you must love God. What does it mean to love God? You may think you need to go to church and sing hymns to love Him, or read the Bible every day. But the Pharisees did all of this and God rebuked them. They prayed and read the Scriptures, memorizing all of it. They didn't love God because they did not know His will.

One day Jesus was invited to the Pharisees' house where they asked to eat with him. A sinful lady brought an alabaster flask of ointment, wet with her tears. She wiped Jesus' feet with her hair and anointed them with the ointment. With this act, her sins were forgiven and she was saved by her faith. Jesus told Simon and the others not only that He is the one who forgives people's sins, but also how to love God. Luke 7:47 states, "For this reason I say to you, her sins, which are many, have been forgiven, for she loved much; but he who is forgiven little, loves little." If you want to love God, your sins are forgiven by repentance. Matthew states,

> Do not judge so that you will not be judged. For in the way you judge, you will be judged; and by your standard of measure, it will be measured to you. Why do you look at the speck that is in your brother's eye, but do not notice the log that is in your own eye? Or how can you say to your brother, 'Let me take the speck out of your eye,' and behold, the log is in your own eye? You hypocrite, first take the log out of your own eye, and then you will see clearly to take the speck out of your brother's eye. (Matt 7:1–5)

We have to take the log out of our own eye before we can take the speck out of others' eyes. It's easy to see others' sins. Whatever we encounter in the media, we should repent. God opens our eyes to other people's sins. When we repent other people's sins, we love God more because we are forgiven more. Those who do not repent end up hating other people. The people who stand in our way will fall away. The Scripture reveals that the way to love God in addition to repentance is to keep His commandments. John 14:21 states, "Whoever has my commandments and keeps them, he it is who loves me. And he who loves me swill be loved by my Father, and I will love him and manifest myself to him."

One of His commandments is "Love your enemies and pray for those persecute you. Then you will become sons of God" (Matt 5:44–48). Is loving your enemies possible? God is a loving God.

God causes His sun to rise on the evil and the good—not just the good—and causes His rain to fall on the righteous and the unrighteous. God loves all people, even the unrighteous and evil. He is patient, waiting for them to return, and He gives them many chances. Christ died for everyone, even the Pharisees and the Romans, those who persecuted the Christians. Therefore, we as followers of Christ should love our enemies. God does not ask us to do impossible things, so we should open our eyes to the Bible. According to Psalms, our life will be better in the presence of our enemies. Psalm 23:5 states, "You prepare a table before me in the presence of my enemies; You have anointed my head with oil; My cup overflows." Recall Galatians 6:7: "Whatever a man sows, this he will also reap." Enemies actually are messengers that God sends us to reveal our ancestors' sins and our own sins. For example, if someone deceives you, you will likely be unhappy and treat that person as an enemy. But this means that either you or your ancestors deceived others before. The person who deceived you has committed sin and will reap what he has sown. In other words, your enemy's life will be miserable due to the sin he or she commits. However, if you repent that sin as yours or belonging to your ancestors, you will receive blessings due to your repentance, which leads to the real blessing from God. God will make your life better in the presence of your enemy. Since that enemy brings blessings from God, even if they harmed you, you can love your enemy rather than hating them. If you give in to your enemies, that is, if you are distressed, anxious, or angered by them, you lose. Instead you should win over them and love them, so that God will prepare you a table before them and anoint you. If a situation arises that blocks you, you should have love so that you can overcome and know that you will move onto something better.

Joseph's brothers were very wise in their own eyes "killing" Joseph. However, they had to live in regret and fear when they met Joseph again. Without Joseph's forgiveness, they would not survive. Unlike his brothers, Joseph was a man of forgiveness. Joseph said to them, "Do not fear, for am I in the place of God? As for you, you meant evil against me, but God meant it for good, to bring it about that many people should be kept alive, as they are today. So do not fear; I will provide for you and your little ones" (Gen 50:19–21).

In order to live in health, you should overcome all enemies, which give you much stress. Eat the best medicine every day, which is the promise of Lord. Enemies are not just people with swords; everything in the world is an enemy that you could be afraid of. We cannot lose to our enemies. Instead, repent and overcome. Look toward God in every situation until you become sons of God. He will reward you. Even if you repented yesterday, you may fall today. If you do not repent, you may fall. What if you are already sick? Seek the Lord faithfully and trust in the promise of God:

> And He said, "If you will give earnest heed to the voice of the Lord your God, and do what is right in His sight, and give ear to His commandments, and keep all His statutes, I will put none of the diseases on you which I have put on the Egyptians; for I, the Lord, am your healer. (Exod 15:26)

Since the Lord is your healer, He will restore your health. I testified about my severe asthma, which went away after I repented my sins. I also witnessed many healings with the mystery of Christ. When my wife was pregnant with our second daughter, she suffered from anemia. However, her anemia was healed and she gave birth to our daughter without complications. I also observed an amazing healing from the Lord. I witnessed a newborn whose left leg looked abnormal. Her leg moved freely back and forth rather than bending in one direction. Her mom's gynecologist could not explain the symptom. However, the Almighty healing power came upon the baby and her leg was healed. Sometimes, God allows you to experience troubles so that you can overcome and be worthy of the kingdom of God, holding onto God steadfastly through anything and everything.

> This is a plain indication of God's righteous judgment so that you will be considered worthy of the kingdom of God, for which indeed you are suffering. For after all it is only just for God to repay with affliction those who afflict

you, and to give relief to you who are afflicted and to us as well when the Lord Jesus will be revealed from heaven with His mighty angels in flaming fire, dealing out retribution to those who do not know God and to those who do not obey the gospel of our Lord Jesus. (2 Thess 1:5–8)

If you have illnesses, place that burden onto God, and He will bear it: "Blessed be the Lord, who daily bears our burden. The God who is our salvation" (Ps 68:19).

CHAPTER 4

MYSTERY OF GODLINESS

LORD AND CHRIST

IN the Old Testament, Daniel's story is very interesting. In his youth, he was selected to serve Nebuchadnezzar, king of Babylon. He became a respected leader under Darius, the king of Babylon. However, other officers were jealous of his power and wanted to get rid of him. Because Daniel was so faithful, there was no laziness or dishonesty to be found in him. The only way to trap Daniel was to use his faith against him. The other officials went to Darius requesting a new law. According to the new law, for thirty days, no one was allowed to worship any god or man other than Darius. Anyone who disobeyed the new law would be thrown into the lions' den. However, even knowing the new law, Daniel did not give up worshiping God three times a day. The high officials and the governors accused Daniel of violating the new law and cast him into the lions' den. Even though Darius tried to save Daniel, the high officials insisted that law could not be changed. God sent His angel and shut the lions' mouths to protect Daniel. He was completely unharmed.

From this story, you might think Daniel was a special person in front of God. But why does the Bible include this story? The Bible is not a fable, but truth. The Scripture shows us how we can live as men of God. Daniel had special wisdom and understanding from God (Dan 1:17, 20). There are two types of wisdom: the wisdom of God and the wisdom of the world. We cannot come to know God through the wisdom of the world (1 Cor 1:21). The wisdom of the world is earthly, arrogant, jealous, selfish, ambitious, and demonic (Jas 3: 14–16). Compared to this, the wisdom of God is pure, peaceful, gentle, reasonable, full of mercy and good fruits, unwavering, and without hypocrisy (Jas 3: 17–18). According to Proverbs, the humble will follow the humble. "When pride comes, then comes dishonor, but with the humble is wisdom" (Prov 11:2).

In other words, Daniel was a humble person. In addition to his humility, Daniel received favor from the Lord. How do we receive great favor like Daniel? Let's examine his life more closely. Proverbs 8:35 states, "For he who finds me finds life and obtains favor from the Lord." However, people constantly try to gain wealth and make a name for themselves. What we need to have is favor from the Lord by turning from our iniquity and giving attention to the truth.

Proverbs 22:1 states, "A good name is to be more desired than great wealth, favor is better than silver and gold." Daniel looked for favor from the Lord. He loved God even when his life was in danger. Even though he could have been killed, Daniel did not stop to kneel and pray before God. Enemies tried to kill Daniel, who held a high position while his people were captive under Babylon. Thanks to favor from the Lord, Daniel not only survived, but also was able to reveal the glory of God in front of all the nations, including his enemies. More importantly, Daniel remembered the promise of God and repented his ancestors' sins as his own:

> I prayed to the Lord my God and confessed and said, "Alas, O Lord, the great and awesome God, who keeps His covenant and lovingkindness for those who love Him and keep His commandments, we have sinned committed iniquity, acted wickedly and rebelled, even turning aside from Your commandments and ordinances. Moreover, we have not listened to Your servants the prophets, who spoke in Your name to our kings, our princes, our fathers and all the people of the land. (Dan 9:4–6)

The Israelites turned away from God and couldn't understand their sins, living however they wanted, which is why calamities befell them. However, Daniel repented those iniquities and asked for the mercy of the Lord. The prayer God desires is repentance. To seek good and to know God—that is how you gain favor. If you have favor from God, no matter where you go, you will do well. You must constantly seek His favor, because that is how you understand the truth (Dan 9:13). You prosper with His favor, but you need to gain wisdom first. Wisdom is gained by repentance with thanksgiving. Even if you do not encounter any dangers, you need God's favor to overcome all kinds of problems in your daily life. God wants to be our helper, but people do not receive help from the Lord. You cannot see your own future, so because you try to live your own life, you constantly run into problems. However, there is good news. Hebrews 13:6 states, "so that we confidently say, "THE LORD IS MY HELPER, I WILL NOT BE AFRAID. WHAT WILL MAN DO TO ME?" When the Lord is your helper, you are unafraid and live a victorious life.

In the Apostle's Creed, it says that Christ suffered under Pontius Pilate, was crucified, and buried. It states that Pontius Pilate and the Romans killed Him, but in Acts 2:36–41, it says that the entire House of Israel crucified Him. Not just the Romans, but all of Israel. Even today, we think that we couldn't have killed Him. But the Israelites killed Him and were pierced to the heart. As sinners, we killed Christ. However, God made Jesus both Lord and Christ.

> Therefore let all the house of Israel know for certain that God made Him both Lord and Christ-this Jesus whom you crucified. (Acts 2:36)

Instead of destroying the Israelites who killed His only begotten Son, God gave us a Lord and Christ. When Israelites heard this message, they asked Apostle Peter, "What shall we do?" Peter said to them, "repent and each of you be baptized in the name of Jesus Christ for the forgiveness of your sins; and you will receive the gift of the Holy Spirit" (Acts 2:37–38). When you repent, Christ and the Lord as your helper will be with you. Christ forgives us our sins. In verse 37, the Israelites' hearts were pierced and they repented with the blood of Christ (Eph. 1:7). Why do people believe in Jesus? Some will say it is because they want to go to Heaven, but while we are on earth, we should also receive help from the Lord. Without help from the Lord, people live on their own. As Proverbs reveals, people ruin their own way:

> The foolishness of man ruins his way, And his heart rages against the Lord. (Prov 19:3)

Many people do not understand why God made Jesus both Lord and Christ. Because many do not know the Lord and Christ, they keep calling for Jesus alone. That is why church goers do not know the Lord is their helper. Instead of getting help from their helper, unfortunately, they spend their lives worrying even if they attend worship services regularly and read the Bible. They also think that the Lord is with them in all circumstances. If the Lord is with them, why the Lord does not protect them from accidents, disasters, or diseases? Grace is when the Lord is with us (Luke 1:28). That is why we need grace from the Lord all the time. Grace/favor is turning from our iniquity and giving attention to the truth. One of the hardest things to do is turn away from iniquity. Bad habits are not easily corrected. In the same way, it's hard to leave our sins, the sins of the heart and flesh. The Law was given through Moses (John 1:17). Why was the Law given? The Pharisees tried to keep the Law; in fact, they kept the Law best. They knew exactly what they had to do. But Romans 3:20 says that the Law was given to us in order for us to realize our sins. In Eden, Adam and Eve didn't need the Law because they lived with God. Because of sin, they were chased out. People do not know how to understand their sins through the Law. We should do this day and night. Grace and truth are realized through Jesus Christ. Not given, but realized. If you do not receive these, you do not receive salvation. Ephesians 2:5 states, "even when we were dead in our wrongdoings, made us alive together with Christ (by grace you have been saved)."

Grace is salvation. So, the Lord has to be with you in order for you to receive salvation. Without the Lord, how can you have grace? Many people in the Bible who were once believers left the Lord. Saul believed in God and was made king, but the Lord was no longer with him. Why? King Saul did not obey God, choosing to follow his own path. Since Saul was humble, God chose him to be Israel's king, but afterward he became arrogant and rejected the word of the Lord, so Saul and his family and his country all died. Many churches claim that once you are blessed, you keep your blessing. Saul was blessed, but ultimately committed suicide. If you reject the word of the Lord, then the Lord will reject you from being exalted, like Saul. King Solomon was also blessed and favored by the Lord. 1 Chronicles states,

> Then all Israel gathered to David at Hebron and said, "Behold, we are your bone and your flesh. In times past, even when Saul was king, you were the one who led out and brought in Israel; and the Lord your God said to you, 'You shall shepherd My people Israel, and you shall be prince over My people Israel.' (1 Chr 11:1-2)

Solomon was a son of David, and David was blessed, so he passed his blessings on to Solomon. Solomon was extremely blessed, and when God asked him what he wanted, Solomon answered 'wisdom.' He humbled himself before God, saying that he was like a child and didn't know what to do. God granted him wisdom. At the time, Israel was enemies with Moab and Ammon, who were descendants of Lot. 1 Kings 11:5 states, "For Solomon went after Ashtoreth the goddess of the Sidonians and after Milcom the detestable idol of the Ammonites." The Moabites and Ammonites all believed in God, and their ancestors were Lot's daughters, who were saved from Sodom and Gomorrah. But because they turned away from the Lord, they started worshipping other gods, just as Solomon did. We must hold onto the Lord until the end.

Compared to the Pharisees who were so devout to keep laws and separated themselves from sinners, David who killed Uriah so he could take his wife, Bathsheba, was ethically worse than the Pharisees. David was a murderer and an adulterer, but God didn't kill him because he repented. Lot could have been blessed because of Abram, but he sinned and turned away from God. People who admitted that they were sinners came to John the Baptist and later became followers of Jesus Christ. However, the Pharisees judged John the Baptist, labeling him a demon-possessed man, and they claimed Jesus used demons when He healed many people. Although the Pharisees all believed in God, they were not blessed or exalted. They were not even justified by the Lord (Luke 18:14).

We need grace to be blessed. Until then, the only thing we can do is repent with the blood of Christ. Even if people jeer at us or hate us, we should repent to the end. Through repentance, we receive favor from the Lord and He becomes our helper.

WHAT IS GODLINESS?

During the great flood of the Old Testament, only Noah and his seven family members survived. How could a loving God kill the rest of the world? Do you think only Noah and his family believed in God at that time? Do you think the rest of world rejected the Lord? Let's examine the Scripture. According to 2 Peter 2:5, God brought a flood upon the world of the ungodly. In verse 6, Sodom and Gomorrah were also destroyed because of ungodliness. What is godliness, and how can we avoid ungodliness? According to James 1:27, godliness is to help orphans and widows, and secondly, keep oneself unstained by the world. How do you keep yourself unstained by the world? Romans 1:18 states, "For the wrath of God is revealed from heaven against all ungodliness and unrighteousness of men who suppress the truth in unrighteousness." The wrath of God is visited on the ungodly: plagues, disasters, illnesses. 1 John 2:15–16 says not to love the world nor the things in the world. Many say that they can love God and not the things in the world, but God is not deceived. Things of the world include the lust of the flesh, the foods you eat, things you want to buy. It's not that these are bad, but if you love these too much, you love them more than God. Furthermore, the boastful pride of life refers to boasting about your accomplishments. When God calls you, it does not matter what you've achieved or earned. You cannot take money with you when you leave this world.

So how do we live a godly life? We must keep ourselves un-stained by the world, loving God rather than the things of the world. How do we do that? We are easily tempted. Telling an alcoholic not to drink does not guarantee they won't fall again. The only way to avoid being stained by the world is to repent the sins coming out of our hearts and flesh, especially the love of money, which is a root of all sorts of evil. You must also repent the sins which make you ungodly. Why did Christ die and shed blood for us? Because we were ungodly (Rom 5:6).

If you repent with the blood of Christ, you are free from un-godliness. Being able to live happily is a blessed life, rather than a life beset by problems. The only way out is Christ. What sins must you repent to be godly? Jude describes the characteristics of ungodly people:

> To execute judgment upon all, and to convict all the un-godly of all their ungodly deeds which they have done in an ungodly way, and of all the harsh things which ungodly sinners have spoken against Him." These are grumblers, finding fault, following after their own lusts; they speak arrogantly, flattering people for the sake of gaining an advantage. (Jude 1:15–16)

People think that if they just go to church and believe, they are righteous. However, have you never grumbled after you con-fessed Jesus as your Savior? Have you not found others at fault after you became Christian? There is a gap between the teaching of the Bible and church doctrine. You must follow the teaching of the Scripture. In other words, you must repent these sins so that you do not end up being ungodly. More specifically, we must re-pent grumbling and complaining, speaking arrogantly, following after our own lusts, and flattering people for the sake of gaining an advantage. Even if you repented yesterday, you can lose your thanksgiving today. With thanksgiving we must remain alert. That is why we must "pray without ceasing" (1 Thess 5:17). Colossians 4:2 states, "Devote yourselves to prayer, keeping alert in it with an attitude of thanksgiving." You stay awake with thanksgiving, so if you lose thanksgiving, you are no longer alert.

Recall the story of Lot. In Genesis 19:14, Abraham knew of the destruction of Sodom and Gomorrah, so he petitioned God, bargaining for Him to save the city. Lot also knew but his sons-in-law thought that he was joking. When God calls us, that is the end of our time here on earth. Lot's own family did not take him seriously. Those cities were made an example for those who would be ungodly, so we should be on the alert. Lot was rescued by God, but his wife turned back and was turned into a pillar of salt (Gen 19:26). When the Lord comes back to call us, we go before Him no matter who we are or how old we are. Many receive the word but do not follow it the same way, like Lot's sons-in-law or the people Noah warned. If you do not repent, what you see and hear will erode your righteous soul, even if you have achieved righteousness.

In Jude 1:18–19, those who are devoid of the Spirit are ungodly, but believers claim they have the Spirit. If you depart from the Spirit, you become a perishable beast. The wicked will be removed like dross (Ps 119:119). The ones who fall to destruction are not more sinful. If you do not repent, you will also fall. Those in the church who speak falsehoods think that because God is a loving God, whoever goes to church will be saved. This is untrue. We should live godly lives before the Lord, and no one can live our lives for us. Matthew states,

> For the coming of the Son of Man will be just like the days of Noah. For as in those days before the flood they were eating and drinking, marrying and giving in marriage, until the day that Noah entered the ark, and they did not understand until the flood came and took them all away; so will the coming of the Son of Man be. (Matt 24:37–39)

When the Lord returns, it will be like the time of Noah. Verse 42 says to be on the alert because we do not know when the Lord will return. What the Lord desires is for us to be godly and awake, to pay attention. 2 Peter explains, and if He rescued righteous Lot, oppressed by the sensual conduct of unprincipled men (for by what he saw and heard that righteous man, while living among them, felt his righteous soul tormented day after day by their lawless deeds, (2 Pet 2:7–8)

People see and hear but do not repent. Demons do their work in the sons of wrath. The demons you see in media can corrode your soul. 2 Peter also states,

then the Lord knows how to rescue the godly from temptation, and to keep the unrighteous under punishment for the day of judgment, and especially those who indulge the flesh in its corrupt desires and despise authority. (2 Pet 2:9–10)

God was patient with Sodom and Gomorrah, giving them many chances. If you are not godly, you will be caught in mishaps and problems. If we live righteously, we will not fall into problems or stumble from temptation. It looks like the Lord's promise is very slow to be completed. However, the Lord is patient toward you, "not wishing for any to perish but for all to come to repentance" (2 Pet 3:8–9).

GODLY MAN CORNELIUS

There was a man at Caesarea named Cornelius, a centurion of what was called the Italian cohort, a devout man and one who feared God with all his household, and gave many alms to the Jewish people and prayed to God continually (Acts 10:1–2). Even though Cornelius was a foreigner, he believed in God. He was devout and repented with his family. One day, Cornelius saw an angel of God in a vision (Acts 10:3). When we pray every day, we don't have to be disappointed if God does not answer. One day, God will answer our prayer when the time is right. It doesn't have to be in the form of an angel. It is often in the form of other people or works. Meeting people seems coincidental, but it's not. How were Cornelius's prayers answered? Acts 10:4 records, "And fixing his gaze on him and being much alarmed, he said, "What is it, Lord?" And he said to him, "Your prayers and alms have ascended as a memorial before God." Eventually Cornelius's prayers led to the Apostle Peter and opened Peter' eyes.

This scripture shows how Cornelius's prayers ascended to the Lord as a memorial before God. The two key words are godliness and fear of the Lord. After Peter met with Cornelius, he realized that God welcomes anyone who is right and fears Him (Acts 10: 34–35). The Israelites claimed that they were the chosen people. If the Israelites associated with a foreigner, they said it was unlawful, unholy or unclean (Acts 10:28). However, Peter obeyed God's command to meet Cornelius, a godly man, and learned that foreigners and Jews are brothers and sisters in the Lord. God said that only those who were chosen obtained what Israel was seeking, and the rest were hardened. Romans reveals,

> What then? What Israel is seeking, it has not obtained, but those who were chosen obtained it, and the rest were hardened; just as it is written, "GOD GAVE THEM A SPIRIT OF STUPOR, EYES TO SEE NOT AND EARS TO HEAR NOT, DOWN TO THIS VERY DAY. (Rom 11:7)

There are two types of people: the chosen and the hardened. What does it mean to be hardened? If you do not repent the sins from your heart, you become hardened. Some people pray but only ask things of God or pray out of habit. They do not expect God to answer. Why? Even if they pray, only the chosen obtain what they are seeking. Sometimes you repent but it does not seem like God hears you. Of course, if you pray for your own benefit, God will disregard it. Even more, if you turn away your ear from listening to the Law which tells your sins (Rom 3:20), your prayer is an abomination (Prov 28:9). How do we become the chosen? How do we go the way of the blessed? The way is godliness. Psalm 4:3 states, "But know that the Lord has set apart the godly man for Himself; The Lord hears when I call to Him." Who are the chosen? When you call to Him and receive, you are a godly person. Ephesians states, just as He chose us in Him before the foundation of the world, that we would be holy and blameless before Him. In love He predestined us to adoption as sons through Jesus Christ to Himself, according to the kind intention of His will, to the praise of the glory of His grace, which He freely bestowed on us in the Beloved. (Eph 1:4–6)

Before God made the world, He had chosen us in Christ, not just the Israelites. The Israelites were arrogant, saying that they were the chosen ones. Godliness and being chosen are all in Christ. To be chosen means you are in Christ. Some theologians defined predestination as God choosing certain people. But God chose godly men in Christ. Many believe that people are predestined to go to Heaven, but their prayers are hardly heard. Why do people meet with death and destruction? It is not because they were predestined. You can be chosen in Christ. You go in Christ with thanksgiving, but because you cannot give thanks in all circumstances, you have to repent. With repentance and thanksgiving, you enter Christ and then you have faith, becoming the chosen.

Those who are godly are washed with the blood of Christ. If you are godly, you abide in Him. Even if you are in Christ, if you sin and your heart becomes hardened, you are once again outside of Christ. So those who are godly abide in Christ without leaving. If you continue to abide in Christ, God will hear your prayers, and you will become chosen, of His people. People do not know whether they are in Christ or not. Abram left his father's house because God commanded him, but he ran into a wasteland and fell. He repented and once again followed God. He told Pharaoh that Sarai was his sister in order to save his life, thinking that they would kill him and take her. He desired an heir and had Ishmael by his servant Hagar. Abraham fell again and again. If you do not repent, your life will reflect Abram's, with many ups and downs. People who attend church say that they love God, but they also love the world, which is against God. However, God loves us and takes mercy on us even if we leave Christ. He is patient and waits for us. Galatians 3:29 reveals, "And if you belong to Christ, then you are Abraham's descendants, heirs according to promise." The Israelites boasted of being descendants of Abraham, because everyone else was a Gentile. But here it explains that if you are in Christ, you are a descendant of Abraham and heirs according to promise. Outside of Christ, your heart becomes hardened. If you love the world, you have no faith in God and end up with many regrets. People often look at their lives and lament. Outside of Christ, we are plagued with anxieties and concerns, grumbling and complaining. If you are disappointed in your situation, do not worry. Since God has promised you, it will be done. Romans states,

> Without becoming weak in faith he contemplated his own body, now as good as dead since he was about a hundred years old, and the deadness of Sarah's womb; yet, with respect to the promise of God, he did not waver in unbelief but grew strong in faith, giving glory to God, and being fully assured that what God had promised, He was able also to perform. (Rom 4:19–21)

Why did God promise Abraham a son, only for it to take 25 years? At first, Abraham and Sarah doubted God's promise. Because our hearts do not wholly trust in the promise of God, blessings can take a while. Sometimes it takes time to receive from the Lord, until you are qualified to receive what you want. Once Abraham was assured of God's promise, then God was able to perform. You have no reason to falter because God is Almighty and will do according to His promise. We must believe that we will prosper because God promised. Don't look around and lose your faith. If you falter, it will take longer. If you hold onto your faith, God will bless you.

PURE AND UNDEFILED GODLINESS

Psalm 32 starts with a statement: "How blessed is he whose transgression is forgiven, Whose sin is covered!" When you confess your transgression to the Lord and acknowledge your sins, the Lord will forgive your transgressions and sins. Psalm 32:6 assures, "Therefore, let everyone who is godly pray to You in a time when

You may be found; Surely in a flood of great waters they will not reach him." Here it says 'godly.' If you keep repenting, you become godly. There are sins that you commit that you don't know about, or that you have forgotten, things too old for you to remember.

However, there are also sins your forefathers committed, which is transgression. God reminds you of these things so that you can repent. If you become a godly person, you can meet the Lord. If you pray to Him in a time when He may be found, then you can meet the Lord your helper. Even in great floods, you will be protected. He will protect you from all destruction. People were destroyed by the great flood because of their ungodliness. The Almighty God is a loving, kind, merciful, and patient Lord. According to Psalm 25:19, God gives lovingkindness and truth to everyone who keeps His covenant and His testimonies. To the Lord, a thousand years is like one day (2 Pet 3:8). If we take two thousand years to return to the Lord, to Him, only two days have passed. The Lord is patient with us. What we need is the blood of Christ to be a godly person. 2 Peter warns,

> But the day of the Lord will come like a thief, in which the heavens will pass away with a roar and the elements will be destroyed with intense heat, and the earth and its works will be burned up. (2 Pet 3:10)

What God wants from us is repentance. Jesus' first message was repentance. If you do not repent, you are open to destruction. God gave the New Covenant to the Israelites because they left the Old Covenant. He gave them a new chance. He wants us to have His lovingkindness and truth. However, many people do not know about washing their sins and transgressions with the blood of Christ. There are false beliefs that deceive, and demons who block out the light of Christ. Receiving grace once does not last forever. David, as an anointed king, sinned by killing Uriah and taking his wife for himself. King David acknowledged his sin and repented what he committed. However, because of his sin, his baby died. Later on, his own son, Absalom, betrayed him. He had to flee from Jerusalem to avoid Absalom's attack. Though believers can return with repentance, the wage of sin is enormous. It is better not to face those disasters if possible. The Scripture tells us how to avoid them.

The Pharisees knew the Scriptures and were very respected, but Jesus called them vipers and hypocrites:

> Either make the tree good and its fruit good, or make the tree bad and its fruit bad; for the tree is known by its fruit. You brood of vipers, how can you, being evil, speak what is good? For the mouth speaks out of that which fills the heart. (Matt 12:33–34)

Why were the Pharisees poisonous? James 3 says,

> But no one can tame the tongue; it is a restless evil and full of deadly poison. With it we bless our Lord and Father, and with it we curse men, who have been made in the likeness of God; from the same mouth come both blessing and cursing. My brethren, these things ought not to be this way. (Jas 3:8–10)

The tongue is a restless evil and a deadly poison. The tongue is not inherently evil, but it speaks what is in the heart, and out of the heart comes sins such as evil thoughts and not wanting to do the will of God. God says that He will fill us, but we have to know how. Poison comes from the heart, so those who do not clean their hearts, even if they say they love God, poison others. Destruction and misery are in their paths (Rom 3:16). Recall Matthew 15:19. Church goers do not know how to clean their hearts. They are the equivalent of today's Pharisees.

What is better: to prevent misfortune before it happens or to cry out to the Lord when you encounter despair in your life? According to Proverbs, you will be satisfied with what your lips produce:

> With the fruit of a man's mouth his stomach will be satisfied; He will be satisfied with the product of his lips. Death and life are in the power of the tongue, And those who love it will eat its fruit. (Prov 18: 20–21)

Your tongue is a powerful tool that decides between death and life. Whatever you say, you will eat those words. You will be filled with satisfaction in whatever you say when you clean your heart with the blood of Christ. Thus, if you say good things, you will eat those good things and will be satisfied with them. This is God's promise.

When the Lord commanded Moses to scout the land of Canaan, there were two very different reports. Only Caleb and Joshua among the twelve heads of their tribes brought back a positive report: "it certainly does flow with milk and honey" (Num 14:27). The others considered themselves as grasshoppers, and led the Israelites into distress and hopelessness. They grumbled against Moses and Aaron, despised the promise of God, and eventually were not allowed to enter the Promised Land. Psalms 107 warns,

> There were those who dwelt in darkness and in the shadow of death, Prisoners in misery and chains, Because they had rebelled against the words of God And spurned the counsel of the Most High. (Ps 107:10–11)

It is unfortune that the Israelites did not trust the word of God and rejected the promise of the Lord with their own lips. They chose death with their tongues. Those Israelites witnessed so many miracles of God. They were a baptized congregation. They ate spiritual food and drank spiritual drink. However, they all died in the wilderness without entering the Promised Land. They were all baptized into Moses in the cloud and in the sea, and they were part of this congregation in the wilderness. The Israelites did not have faith in God before and during the Exodus, but after they gained faith, they were baptized. So, were they saved? Even after the Israelites witnessed signs and the glory of God, they disobeyed God's voice and tested Him.

> Surely all the men who have seen My glory and My signs which I performed in Egypt and in the wilderness, yet have put Me to the test these ten times and have not listened to My voice, shall by no means see the land which I swore to their fathers, nor shall any of those who spurned Me see it. (Num 14: 22–23)

Although they had faith and were baptized, God was not pleased with most of them. They craved evil things. You must become people who please God and men. That does not mean that you will be perfect and make everyone happy. King David was not perfect, but he held onto God and kept repenting his sins. God is patient and waits for us to repent. How can you please God? By serving Christ: "For he who in this way serves Christ is acceptable to God and approved by men" (Rom 14:18). What does 'serving Christ' mean? It means to clean our sins with the blood of Christ, leading to godliness.

Christ was crucified so that He could become the Christ and our Lord (Acts 2:36). People call out to the Lord without truly understanding why Jesus was crucified. To be godly in front of the Lord, you must first repent your sins and transgressions with the blood of Christ. Secondly, you should be satisfied with the fruit of your mouth. Thirdly, you must keep yourself unstained by the world, a life pleasing God. God delights in godly persons (Ps 16:3), which is how you should live. You should not only go to church, but become like the saints. Then, He will delight in you. God does not wish any to die, but to repent and gain salvation (2 Pet 3:8–9). The only way to please God is to repent with the blood of Christ and to live like saints. 1 Timothy 2:3 reads, "this is good and acceptable in the sight of God our Savior." This is what God accepts, not just worship, because even demons can worship. Churches believe that if they gather and worship and praise Him, God will accept it. He does not receive hymns without repentance. When King Saul was haunted by a demon, David went and played music for him to quiet the demon. Even demons enjoy music. If you grumble and complain, you cannot please God. On the contrary, you violate the will of God, which is thanksgiving in all circumstances. 1 Corinthians warns,

> Nor grumble, as some of them did, and were destroyed by the destroyer. Now these things happened to them as an example, and they were written for our instruction, upon whom the ends of the ages have come. (1 Cor 10:10–11)

These things were written as an example so that you would not fall. Going to church alone will not save you.

If you repent, God will forgive. That is why the blood of Christ is an amazing thing. God wants everyone to gain salvation. When you live a godly life and keep repenting sins of ungodliness, God will lift you out of the trials you face. We have fallen prey to demons and have failed to understand the word of God. Let us become godly now and glorify God, so that we can receive blessings. In Christ the head of our church, let us depart from the ungodly path and instead receive His blessings and promise. If you forget the word of God or the promise of God like the Israelites, then everything you do will be beset by curse and pestilence. Deuteronomy presages,

> The Lord will send upon you curses, confusion, and rebuke, in all you undertake to do, until you are destroyed and until you perish quickly, on account of the evil of your deeds, because you have forsaken Me. The Lord will make the pestilence cling to you until He has consumed you from the land where you are entering to possess it. The Lord will smite you with consumption and with fever and with inflammation and with fiery heat and with the sword and with blight and with mildew, and they will pursue you until you perish. The heaven which is over your head shall be bronze, and the earth which is under you, iron. The Lord will make the rain of your land powder and dust; from heaven it shall come down on you until you are destroyed (Deut 28:20–24).

Diseases are a result of sin. People are not taught the way to righteousness because they think if they believe in Jesus they are righteous. Why then are they met with destruction? God gives them problems so that they can become His children (2 Thess 1:5). When you have problems, you should give thanks with repentance because right now you are not worthy of God's kingdom and are holding onto things of the world. You must believe Christ to be a righteous person (Phil 3:9). What does it mean to believe in Christ? It means to repent with the blood of Christ. You must believe in the mystery of Christ, acknowledge your sins, and wash them until you give thanks in all circumstances. Once you become righteous (1 Cor 1:30), God will protect you from all evil. Romans 1:18–19 states, "For the wrath of God is revealed from heaven against all ungodliness and unrighteousness of men who suppress the truth in unrighteousness, because that which is known about God is evident within them; for God made it evident to them."

The wrath of God is visited on the ungodly: plagues, disasters, illnesses. You must be godly by keeping unstained by the world. Telling an alcoholic not to drink does not guarantee they won't fall again. Even if you tell yourself not to do it, it's hard to keep yourself from being tempted. Why did Christ die and shed blood for us? Because we were ungodly (Rom 5:6). The only way to be godly and maintain godliness is the mystery of Christ, which is repentance with the blood of Christ. It is up to you whether you decide to live a pure, undefiled and godly life.

CHAPTER 5

THE MYSTERY OF CHRIST

∙∙

BOASTING IN THE CROSS OF OUR LORD JESUS CHRIST

IN Europe, there is famous cathedral built where St. Peter is buried, a literal definition of building a church on the rock. But few attend church there; it's just a tourist attraction. Many churches in Europe have severely lost congregation members. European churches were once wealthy, able to construct beautiful sanctuaries. People immigrated to America and brought the faith with them, which allowed missionaries to go to Korea where many churches popped up. However, European churches are experiencing regression. Their large buildings are empty or full of tourists, and church buildings are turned into bars or restaurants. Korean churches are not much different. Once, Korean churches boasted the fastest growth in the world. Pastorship was a very popular vocation. However, many people do not respect church pastors any longer and consider them charlatans. People do not trust the church because of church goers' bad behavior and partition. This is a huge loss to the congregations. Their messages are to follow their denomination's teaching rather than deliver the word of God. If any denomination does not agree with their teaching, they judge them as heresy. They do not preach repentance or the blood of

Christ. Since many church goers are taught that they are already saved, they do not feel that they need to attend service or repent their sins. They are bold to commit sins and even fight within the church. In the news, there was a married Korean pastor who slept with a woman in his congregation. Many people think churches are bad places, and this news garnered a lot of hate amongst non-believers. Recently, there was an incident in one of the biggest churches in Seoul, in which church members used emergency fire extinguishers to attack those who did not support their senior pastor. Several people were left injured. As Romans states, many church members have dishonored God:

> You who boast in the Law, through your breaking the Law, do you dishonor God? For "the name of God is blasphemed among the Gentiles because of you," just as it is written. (Rom 2:23–24)

Just as the Korean pastor dishonored God, nonbelievers will not only despise the church but also blaspheme against God. We must become people who gain favor before God and men. That does not mean that we will be perfect and make everyone happy. King David was not perfect, but he held onto God and kept praying. We fall over and over again, but we can overcome with repentance. Instead of glorifying God, the name of God is blasphemed by churches because they do not follow the teaching of the Scripture. Colossians 4:3 states, "praying at the same time for us as well, that God will open up to us a door for the word, so that we may speak forth the mystery of Christ, for which I have also been imprisoned." What the Apostle Paul said was that the only thing to preach is the mystery of Christ, which is to cleanse with the blood of Christ in repentance. Otherwise, we do not hear or understand the word. Paul went around preaching the gospel, but people wouldn't listen because their hearts were dull. By washing your heart with the blood of Christ, the dullness of your heart will be fixed.

In Acts 8, Philip went to the city of Samaria and proclaimed Christ (Acts 8:5–8). What he preached was not a denomination of Christianity, but Christ. Because of that, people were healed of diseases and demons and there was much rejoicing in the city. God has given us the mystery of Christ through the Bible so that we can proclaim it. What the Apostle Paul boasted was the cross of our Lord Jesus Christ, not how beautiful a sanctuary was, how large and successful a congregation was, or how lovely service was. The Apostle Paul confesses what he boasts in Galatians: "But may it never be that I would boast, except in the cross of our Lord Jesus Christ, through which the world has been crucified to me, and I to the world" (Gal 6:14).

According to Ecclesiastes 10:10, a dull axe cannot cut anything. If you wield one, you get tired, so you must sharpen the axe. If you do not sharpen it, you exert too much force but it will not work. How do we sharpen ourselves? Some people think that education is the answer, because you cannot get a good job without education. Without wisdom, people's words will consume them (Eccl 10:12). It is true that wisdom is the key to success. However, there are two types of wisdom: the wisdom of this world and wisdom from God. According to 1 Corinthians 3:19, the wisdom of this world is foolish. The wisdom of this world makes many people arrogant. However, the wisdom from God not only gives you a good and fruitful life, but also equips you to help others. If we are made sharp with wisdom from God, we are able to be productive and to seek the good of our neighbors. How do we get wisdom from God? As 1 Corinthians states,

> but to those who are the called, both Jews and Greeks,
> Christ the power of God and the wisdom of God.
> (1 Cor 1:24)

When we repent with the blood of Christ, which is the mystery of Christ, Christ as wisdom will be with you. That is why the Apostle Paul spoke the mystery and boasted of the cross of our Lord Jesus Christ. And that is why there was so much happiness and healing in the town where Philip went and proclaimed Christ. You are able to come near God by the blood of Christ (Eph 2:13). Not only do we need to gain wisdom, but also we must keep it. The answer is to repent our sins without ceasing (1 Thess 5:17), which leads to humility (Prov 11:2). Humility has to be kept and maintained. In Hosea 13, there is the story of Ephraim. Ephraim was a son of Joseph, along with Manasseh. They gained the blessings of their father. But Ephraim exalted himself and became arrogant. People trembled at his words because he possessed so much power, but Ephraim died because of his idolatry and arrogance. We must maintain our humility and wisdom, otherwise our arrogance will consume us. They will consume our descendants as well. Similarly, the sons of Abraham are Ishmael and Isaac, whose descendants are warring to this day.

Arrogance is very frightening because of what it can do. Solomon's son, Rehoboam, caused division in his country. God will give you wisdom if you repent with the blood of Christ. Then, you are able to do great things because of God's promise. You can prosper in whatever you do, and you have nothing to worry about because eventually you succeed. When God slows down your progress, there is a reason. God is trying to humble you so that you can become more successful later, and so that you are actually qualified for blessings. If an athlete does not train but gets onto a good team, they will not be able to keep up. James 4:10 states, "Humble yourselves in the presence of the Lord, and He will exalt you." If you experience dishonor and hatred from others, it means you have been prideful. If you are angry about someone else's doing, that is a sign that you have arrogance in your heart. If God has given you a sign, what should you do? Repent. That is the only thing you can do.

When people hate and blame one another rather than repent, conflict arises. Saul went from being king to becoming jealous of David. He was so jealous he tried to kill David. If you have feelings of wanting someone else to fail or even die, you have hatred and arrogance in your heart. However, instead of punishing you right away, God waits for you to come back and repent.

Psalm 123:2 states, "Behold, as the eyes of servants look to the hand of their master, As the eyes of a maid to the hand of her mistress, So our eyes look to the Lord our God." God will be patient and wait for you so that you can repent. Those who are helped by God are the blessed (Ps 146:5). You should remember the ways that God helped you. You should write down your testimonies. When Jesus died, many people who had followed Him were no longer there. But the thief on His right repented his sins. Many followed Jesus and listened to His sermons, but they didn't learn. After Jesus returned from the dead, their ears were open, but when Jesus died, they were afraid because they couldn't understand.

If things aren't going well, repent and understand that God is trying to make you into a better vessel. Without repentance, you are prone to complaining. If you do not keep the mystery of Christ, you do not have the wisdom of God and cannot be humble. That is why the Apostle Paul boasted the cross of our Lord Jesus Christ and spoke the mystery of Christ. Proverbs 3:3–4 states, "Do not let kindness and truth leave you; Bind them around your neck, Write them on the tablet of your heart. So you will find favor and good repute in the sight of God and man." Favor in the sight of God is not something we can obtain on our own. The way to embrace kindness and truth is through the blood of Christ. How do you keep from leaving Christ? You must wash your sins with the blood of Christ every day. That is how you keep His wisdom, which is Christ. Around our necks we should bind kindness and truth, and write them on our hearts. That way, they travel with us wherever we go. Psalm 100:3 states, "Know that the Lord Himself is God; It is He who has made us, and not we ourselves; We are His people and the sheep of His pasture."

Matthew 25 talks about the final judgement day, discerning between sheep and goats. On Judgement Day, everything will be exposed, whether you have lived as sheep or goat. If you believe that you are a sheep obedient to your church's teaching, but find out that you are actually a goat, it will be too late. Follow your Shepherd, instead of being a goat that follows their own thoughts and ways. Through repentance with the blood of Christ, we will gain favor and good repute before God and men. The only way to be righteous is through the blood of Christ. No matter how many sins you have built up, with the blood of Christ they are washed away. Isaiah 1:18 states, "Come now, and let us reason together," Says the Lord, "Though your sins are as scarlet, They will be as white as snow; Though they are red like crimson, They will be like wool."

What do you boast? Your fame, your wealth, your education, or your wisdom? Your boasting should be in the mystery of Christ, the wisdom of God. Boasting in the cross of our Lord Jesus Christ leads you to a peaceful and joyful life. God will protect you when you become a sheep in God's pasture. Let us overflow with peace and joy and life.

THE SIGN OF JONAH

Many Pharisees and scribes were amazed at Jesus' teachings and miracles. They badly wanted to know who Jesus really was. As a result, they listened and examined Jesus' sermons very carefully. Most Pharisees were not pleased with Jesus' miracles, especially on the Sabbath. Even though some of the miracles surprised them, the Pharisees and scribes chiefly thought that Jesus defiled the name of God. One day, some of the scribes and Pharisees decided to challenge Him, asking for a sign. Jesus did not say, "of course I can show you miracles, bring the sick, or bring two pieces of bread so I can feed five-thousand people." Instead of the physical signs they wanted to see, Jesus simply told them He had one sign to give them, which was the sign of Jonah: "Then some of the scribes and Pharisees answered Him, saying, Teacher, we want to see a sign from you." However, what He gives them is the sign of Jonah in Matthew:

> But He answered and said to them, "An evil and adulterous generation craves for a sign; and yet no sign will be given to it but the sign of Jonah the prophet; for just as JONAH WAS THREE DAYS AND THREE NIGHTS IN THE BELLY OF THE SEA MONSTER, so will the Son of Man be three days and three nights in the heart of the earth. The men of Nineveh will stand up with this generation at the judgment, and will condemn it because

they repented at the preaching of Jonah; and behold, something greater than Jonah is here. (Matt 12:39–41)

Note the two concerns Jesus raised here: 1) an adulterous generation desiring a sign, and 2) the only sign given which was the sign of Jonah. In order to examine this, let's explore the story of Jonah.

God commanded a man named Jonah to go the city of Nineveh. According to the Book of Jonah, Nineveh was a great city at the time. However, because of its wickedness, God was going to overthrow it. Before destroying the city, God gave the people a chance to repent, the reason why God sent Jonah to warn them. Despite God's bidding, Jonah did not obey God. He got on a ship in order to sail away from what God commanded him to do. God knew where Jonah was. He sent a big storm to warn him against running away. Jonah knew at once why the storm came about, causing him to beg the sailors to throw him into the sea, saving the ship and its crew. So, Jonah was thrown into the sea and immediately the storm stopped. God had already prepared a sea monster to swallow Jonah. Inside the great fish, Jonah prayed and prayed for three days and nights. Jonah gave thanks to God after he repented before Him. God then commanded the fish to spit Jonah out on dry land. The word of God came to Jonah a second time, telling him to go to Nineveh. Populated by 120,000, Nineveh was very large and would take three days for Jonah to cover with his message. This time, Jonah obeyed God. It should have taken a three days' walk to cover the city, yet Jonah went through the city in only one day's walk. He preached the word of the Lord: "forty days and Nineveh will be overthrown." Even though Jonah preached without much love and spoke only to one-third of the city, the people of Nineveh, including the king, believed in God and repented. God then spared Nineveh.

Moving forward, Jesus came with love and passion to preach at the villages of Judea, urging, "Repent, for the kingdom of Heaven is at hand" (Matt 4:17). Unlike the people of Nineveh, people here did not repent. One of the main reasons Jesus performed many miracles was to show people they needed to repent their sins when they saw God's power. Instead, the Pharisees and scribes tried to find fault with Jesus and did not appreciate His miracles. They even suggested that Jesus was using the power of Beelzebub, the ruler of demons. Jesus rebuked the cities:

> Then He began to denounce the cities in which most of His miracles were done, because they did not repent. "Woe to you, Chorazin! Woe to you, Bethsaida! For if the miracles had occurred in Tyre and Sidon which occurred in you, they would have repented long ago in sackcloth and ashes. Nevertheless I say to you, it will be more tolerable for Tyre and Sidon in the day of judgment than for you. And you, Capernaum, will not be exalted to heaven, will you? You will descend to Hades; for if the miracles had occurred in Sodom which occurred in you, it would have remained to this day. Nevertheless I say to you that it will be more tolerable for the land of Sodom in the day of judgment, than for you. (Matt 11:20–24)

According to John 20:30–31, Jesus performed many wonders and showed many signs. John said that "these have been written that you may believe that Jesus is the Christ, the son of God; and that by believing you may have life in His name." In other words, Jesus performed miracles to offer evidence that that He is the Christ, the Messiah. In addition, Jesus tells people that they need to repent their sins in order to receive life, and to be cleansed through the blood of Christ. By refusing to accept Jesus as Christ, the Pharisees and scribes lost their chance to be saved. In the same manner, if we do not repent, there is only the wrath of God upon us in the form of trials, tribulations, and catastrophes; hence, why bad things happen to "good" people. Jonah prayed to the Lord his God from the stomach of the fish (Jon 2:1–10).

Jonah miraculously survived from certain death. How did he survive inside the fish? He repented before God and promised to obey His command. Above all, Jonah gave thanks to the Lord. He was man of good faith, regardless of his circumstances. Jonah ended up in that mess because he disobeyed God's specific command, and he could have complained and cursed his fate. Yet, he gave thanks to God while inside the fish—after repentance.

What changed Jonah's situation? Furthermore, what changed Jonah? The answer is repentance. Even in the worst situation, facing death, he was able to "sacrifice to the Lord with the voice of thanksgiving." That is why Jesus made sure the story of Jonah was placed in the Bible, instead of other signs and wonders. We must continually enter His glorious gate of Heaven with thanksgiving: "Enter His gates with thanksgiving, and His courts with praise. Give thanks to Him; bless His name" (Ps 100:4). To give thanks in everything is God's will for you in Christ Jesus (1 Thess 5:18). This is only possible when you repent your sins.

If you live a life of thanksgiving, then through Christ you will realize grace and truth. Grace is the Lord with you. The favored one is synonymous with grace: "And coming in, he said to her, "Greetings, favored one! The Lord is with you" (Luke 1:28).

No matter where you are, even inside the fish, the Lord will look over you. God says that one soul is most precious. He loves the world. He sent Jonah to Nineveh to try and save them. When Jonah disobeyed the command of God, all kinds of troubles befell him. Jonah ended up in the fish by the mercy of the Lord. If your life is not peaceful, or you do not see any light for your future, Jonah's story is telling you how your life situation can change. Luke states,

> and He said to them, "Thus it is written, that the Christ would suffer and rise again from the dead the third day, and that repentance for forgiveness of sins would be proclaimed in His name to all the nations, beginning from Jerusalem. You are witnesses of these things." (Luke 24:46–48)

The word of God shows that repentance for forgiveness of sins would be proclaimed to all the nations. God has called us as witnesses to proclaim repentance for the forgiveness of sins, which is the sign of Jonah. However, many churches share their denominations and their deeds instead. We have to return to what the Lord commanded. If we hold onto those commandments, we can prosper and live a life that pleases God.

FOUR-STEP REPENTANCE: REPENTING OUR SINS IN A BIBLICAL WAY

When Jesus began to preach, the first message was "repent, for the kingdom of heaven is at hand" (Matt 4:17). In Mark, Jesus proclaimed, "The time is fulfilled, and the kingdom of God is at hand; repent and believe in the gospel" (Mark 1:15). Your heavenly Father knows what you need before you ask Him (Matt 6:8). The message in Thessalonians 5:17, "pray without ceasing," does not mean to ask whatever you want without ceasing. "Pray without ceasing" means you should repent your sins without ceasing. There are many sins from your heart and your flesh, in addition to the sins passed down from your ancestors. As Proverbs states,

> Adversity pursues sinners, But the righteous will be rewarded with prosperity. (Prov 13:21)

Many churches are eager to teach their own doctrines and build their denominations when they send missionaries to other nations, instead of proclaiming repentance for the forgiveness of sins. Jesus did not praise the scribes and Pharisees' proselytizing efforts while traveling around on sea and land. Instead, Jesus condemned them, saying they were making believers twice as much sons of hell as themselves. Without repentance, new believers' lives are vulnerable to all kinds of disasters, which will lead to the betrayal of God. We must go back to Jesus' teaching, the sign of Jonah, the mystery of Christ.

Why did Jonah take three days before giving thanks and witnessing the miracle of God? Jonah did not give thanks to God after he came out the fish. People give thanks when their prayers are answered or when their life is good. Few are able to give thanks when they are in darkness. On the contrary, people will lament their situation. It is not easy to praise the Lord when life gets hard. However, when you repent your disobedience to God, you are able to give thanks to the Lord with realization of His lovingkindness. The Apostle Paul confessed in Ephesians 3:3 that he knew the mystery by revelation and wrote it. So, when you read the Bible, you can understand the mystery of Christ. Do you understand the mystery of Christ? Have you heard of God's mystery? According to Colossians 2:2, God's mystery is Christ Himself. What is Christ and the mystery of Christ? Why does the Bible use the word 'mystery'? It is because we cannot know a mystery by our own understanding. The mystery was made known to the Apostle Paul by revelation, not by his studying or learning. Even though Saul, who later became Paul, was a scholar of the Law, he did not know who Christ was. He even tried to kill believers of Christ. The exact same thing is happening in churches. The mystery of Christ should be known by revelation and not by teaching. When people repent, God will reveal the mystery just as He did to Paul. Many churches, however, are eager to study the Bible rather than hold revival meetings of repentance. Many seminaries focus on theories from their personal understanding, without this revelation. Under the light of the Lord, you clearly understand the mystery of Christ.

What are the steps to repentance? Once again, this can be understood by the light of God. Who can claim to know God's words? It does not matter to God how well we know Scripture, God seeks fruit from us (Matt 7:20). Christ, God's mystery, changed my life when I repented with His blood. The first step to repentance is to recognize your sins. Without recognition of your sins, you cannot confess them. Therefore, it is very important to know what your sins are. The problem is in how you find and remember your sins, which are revealed through the Law. People tend to read a very limited amount of the Bible, and what they do read happens to be their favorite verses. Yet, the "unpopular" verses of the Bible, like those condemning immorality, coveting, hatred, cursing, and wickedness, show us the naked truth that our hearts are, by nature, filled with sin.

It is very important to repent the sins coming from the heart and flesh (Matt 15:19, Rom 1:28–32, & Gal 5:19–21). When you began repenting these sins, God will open your eyes to realize sins that you have never considered your own before.

The second and the third steps of repentance are to confess your sins and repent to God for His forgiveness. According to

Jeremiah 17:1, the sins you commit are carved on the tablet of our hearts, as with a diamond point, and then simultaneously inscribed on the horns of your altars.

> The sin of Judah is written down with an iron stylus;
> With a diamond point it is engraved upon the tablet of
> their heart And on the horns of their altars, (Jer 17:1)

In other words, whenever you disobey the law of God, the record of your transgression is kept on the horn of altars, in front of God, and the exact sin always remembered. These carved sins cannot be erased at all by human efforts. This is primarily because engraving on your soft heart tissues with a diamond tip, as the metaphor goes, would cause severe damage to your heart.

On the second step, you confess the sins which are engraved on the horns of your altar in front of God. Most people do not know that whenever you commit sins, you really hurt God with them: "You have bought Me not sweet cane with money, Nor have you filled Me with the fat of your sacrifices; Rather you have burdened Me with your sins, You have wearied Me with your iniquities" (Isa 43: 24).

Previously, I did not know that my sins were actually a burden to God. I simply repented to seek forgiveness. According to the law in the Old Testament, everything is purified with the blood of animals; there is no forgiveness without the shedding of blood (Heb 9:22). Because Christ has already shed His blood for us, you do not need the blood of animals anymore. Therefore, whenever you confess your sins and repent to God, you have to use the blood of Christ.

In my experience, the third step of the repentance process is very important to heal the wounded heart. The third step is to wash the sins from the altar of your heart. Before learning how to truly repent, I knew repentance was significant to my spiritual life. I often went to the remote mountain abbey to pray. However, even after repenting, I failed to forgive those who hurt me. This step is vital to restore your broken hearts. Almost all Christians know the basic idea of repentance, yet few are familiar with cleansing the sins of their hearts. The sins in your heart cannot be healed with counseling or therapy, only by repentance using the blood of Christ. When you repent the sins engraved on your heart, you will feel true freedom and peace from anger, hatred, anxiety, uneasiness, and all kinds of other burdens. In this healing process, the blood of Christ cures all sicknesses and chronic diseases. Why is it that among those who claim to have repented, that there is so much suffering and dying from cancer and other fatal diseases? Because they either do not understand, or they skip this very important step. When you start to repent sins, you need to remember to forgive others' sins. In order to be forgiven, you first forgive others' sins. "For if you forgive others for their transgressions, your heavenly Father will also forgive you. But if you do not forgive others, then your Father will not forgive your transgressions" (Matt 6:14–15).

The last step of repentance is to give thanksgiving for the forgiveness of our sins. The will of God is to give thanks in everything (1 Thess 5:18). We are unable to give thanks because of unrepented sins. When Jonah expressed his thanks to God after three days in the fish, God gave him a new life. Through the exact same way, the last step, thanksgiving, is the step that will enable you to taste the miraculous work of God. The sign of Jonah, which has been given by Jesus Christ, represents the repentance process.

Have you thought about why Christ suffered and was raised from dead on the third day? What did it happen specifically on the third day and not the fourth, or fifth day? This "third day" also represents a metaphor of our spiritual life, for "the wages of sin is death" (Rom 6:23). Death by the wages of our sins are represented by those three days. Jonah repented after three days, and he thanked God even before God gave him a new life. God then ordered the fish to spew him out.

How do we learn to give thanks in dire situations? We cannot, by our own strength. However, if you repent until you know the will of God and understand why you are in the current situation, you will then possess the strength to thank God. When you give thanks to God in all circumstances, God will work miracles for you, and the Lord will give you a new life, healing, solutions, and whatever you need.

It is critical that you should not miss even one of the four steps; you need all four pieces in order to get answers from God. Interestingly enough, when the Roman soldiers had crucified Jesus Christ, they divided His clothes into four parts. This is not a coincidence; every single letter in the Bible has been approved by God. These four parts symbolize repentance, as the four pieces should fit together as one, the garment of the High Priest. In other words, our sins have divided the garment of the High Priest who is the mediator between God and human beings (1 Tim 2:5). Without the mediator, we cannot come to God. In the same symbolic way, without retuning the four pieces to form the perfect garment of the High Priest, our prayers are meaningless. As sinful people, we will remain inside the fish, in the darkness, with no future, living a cursed life. 2 Corinthians 5:17 states, "Therefore, if anyone is in Christ, he is a new creation; the old has gone, the new has come!" If you still have the same old character, same old mind, same old inclinations, and same old habits, you are not in Christ. When you realize your sins, when you repent of those sins, when you cleanse your sins from the altar of your heart, and when you can give thanks to God, you will be in Christ, which is the mystery of God. Colossians states,

> to whom God willed to make known what is the riches
> of the glory of this mystery among the Gentiles, which is
> Christ in you, the hope of glory. (Col 1:27)

You must be in Christ first, then Christ will be in you. If you want to be close to God, you have to be in Christ first and be brought near by the blood of Christ. Then, all God's promises will be yours. If you stay outside Christ, Satan will attack you. As Ephesians reveals, you will be brought near God by the blood of Christ:

> remember that you were at that time separate from
> Christ, excluded from the commonwealth of Israel, and
> strangers to the covenants of promise, having no hope
> and without God in the world. But now in Christ Jesus

you who formerly were far off have been brought near by
the blood of Christ. (Eph 2:12–13)

In conclusion, when you are in Christ and have Christ in you,
what comes out is the love of Christ. You first must repent the sins
from your hearts and flesh, the ancestral sins attached to you man-
ifesting as fleshly problems. If you repent all of these and replace
them with Christ, out of your mouths come love and praise. Then
God can fill you to the fullness of His promise. Even if you crucified
the passions of the world yesterday with the blood of Christ, they
still come up today. However, when you keep repenting, God will
protect you from all sorts of problems. You are sinners, so you will
fall again and again. Even if you believe, and even if you repent,
what you need to hold onto is the cross, the mystery of Christ.
When you live a life of thanksgiving, through Christ you will see
the Lord's grace and truth. No matter where you are, the Lord will
look over you. There might be obstacles or enemies present in your
life. However, when you believe in the mystery of Christ, four-step
repentance, God causes all things to work together for good. Even
if things don't seem to be working out right now, everything will
turn out well. Your life is a precious one. You have only one life. Do
not waste your chance to be blessed.

Epilogue

....

Do All to the Glory of God

H UMAN beings are noble creatures. You are a unique person in this world. God is calling you as an ambassador for Christ (2 Cor 5:20). Your duty as an ambassador for Christ is to fear God and keep His commandments. Ecclesiastes 12:13–14 shows, "The conclusion, when all has been heard, is: fear God and keep His commandments, because this applies to every person. For God will bring every act to judgment, everything which is hidden, whether it is good or evil." You should learn the fear of the Lord, teach your children and keep the will of God, which is to give thanks in all circumstances. As Deuteronomy states, you should teach your children how to fear the Lord:

> Remember the day you stood before the Lord your God at Horeb, when the Lord said to me, 'Assemble the people to Me, that I may let them hear My words so they may learn to fear Me all the days they live on the earth, and that they may teach their children.' (Deut 4:10)

God promised blessings to those who fear the Lord (Prov 28:14). Life and prosperity go together, while death and adversity go together (Deut 30:15). Because of sin our hearts harden. Our eyes and ears become dull so that we cannot perceive blessings. This is from the word of God. What do we need to do? The starting point is to repent sins from our hearts and flesh (as stated in Matt 15:19, Rom 1:28–32, and Gal 5:19–21).

If you keep repenting these sins, God will surely bless you. Your life will never be the same. Those who hold onto God will continue to prosper, like Joseph, who became prime minister of Egypt. Whoever has the fear of the Lord will prosper wherever they go. Your children will do even better than your own generation because you pass down blessings to them. When we succeed, we should become humble and receive blessings that we cannot even see or hear or imagine. This is a promise from God. After I received this precious gospel, four-step repentance, the mystery of Christ, my whole life changed. I have pursued the profit of the many for their salvation, as shown in 1 Corinthians 10:31–33: "Whether, then, you eat or drink or whatever you do, do all to the glory of God. Give no offense either to Jews or to Greeks or to the church of God; just as I also please all men in all things, not seeking my own profit but the profit of the many, so that they may be saved."

Because of repentance, I was able to help many students who failed academically. Since they did not know how to repent their sins, I repented their sins on my cross. They were able to achieve impossible dreams and were healed from drug and alcohol addictions. I have witnessed so many healings with repentance (Ps 103:3). Four-step repentance is the Biblical way to repent. When you repent, the Almighty God will not only answer your prayer, but also bless your life, so that you can be a source of blessing to your neighbors.

CLOSING PRAYER:

God, thank You for your lovingkindness. Let us repent and wash the sins that come from our hearts and flesh. Let us become godly now and be rescued from trials. Let us daily repent our grumbling and complaining, being arrogant and following after our own lusts. Let us become godly now and glorify You, so that we can receive blessings. In Christ the head of our church, let us depart from the ungodly path, and instead receive Your blessings and promise. Let us wash ourselves so that we may be filled and that we can understand the love of Christ, being able to distribute it to many others. God, let us gain good repute before You and men. Until now, we have ignored this path. Let us instead wear kindness and truth around our necks, and let us be happy and give thanks, being able to give grace to everyone around us. Let us hate evil and keep the word in our hearts. In Jesus' name we pray, Amen.

www.ingramcontent.com/pod-product-compliance
Lightning Source LLC
Chambersburg PA
CBHW071050090426
42737CB00013B/2309